Outdoor Guide to Using Your GPS

Steve Feathe

CREATIVE
PUBLISHING
international

CHANHASSEN, MINNESOTA

www.creativepub.com

President/CEO: Michael Eleftheriou
Vice President/Publisher: Linda Ball
Vice President/Retail Sales & Marketing: Kevin Haas
Executive Editor, Outdoor Group: Barbara Harold
Creative Director: Brad Springer
Project Manager: Tracy Stanley
Photo Editor: Angela Hartwell
Director, Production Services: Kim Gerber
Production Manager: Laura Hokkanen

Printed on American paper by R. R. Donnelley
10 9 8 7 6 5 4 3 2 1

Outdoor Guide to Using Your GPS
by Steve Featherstone

Cover Photos by: Cover Photography © 2004: top left: Diane Meyer; top right: courtesy
  Alumacraft Boat Company, www.alumacraft.com; bottom left: Nels Akerlund;
  bottom right: Brad Herndon.

Contributing Manufacturers:

  GPS Outfitters, Inc., P.O. Box 237, Stephens City, VA 22655.
  1-800-477-4868. www.gpsoutfitters.com

  Maptech, 10 Industrial Way, Amesbury, MA 01913. 978-792-1000.
  www.maptech.com provided maps on these pages: 67 (both), 71 (bottom), 81, 82, 83, 84, 90,
  91, 99, 102, 105, 106, 130 (both), 138 (top and middle).

  Garmin International, 9875 Widmer Road, Lenexa, KS 66215. 1-800-800-1020.
  www.garmin.com provided the map on page 122.

  National Geographic Maps, P.O. Box 4537, Evergreen, CO 80437-4357. 1-800-962-1643.
  www.nationalgeographic.com provided both maps on page 136.

  Library of Congress Cataloging-in-Publication Data

Featherstone, Steve
  Outdoor guide to using your GPS : tips for hikers, campers, hunters, boaters
  by Steve Featherstone.
      p. cm.
  Includes index.
  ISBN 1-58923-145-7 (sc)
  1. Outdoor recreation--Equipment and supplies. 2. Orienteering--Equipment and
  supplies. 3. Global Positioning System. I. Title.
  GV191.623.F43 2004
  910'.285--dc22

TABLE OF CONTENTS

Introduction

Technological innovation is a double-edged sword. The promise of greater convenience, safety and efficiency always seems to come at ever-greater costs—mainly, our valuable time. Computers are a good example of this trade-off. No one would say we're better off without computers; but few could say that owning a computer or using one at work has given them more time with their family and less time at work.

In fact, the opposite seems to be true. We spend more time than ever, at home and at work, learning various software programs and network configurations, and waiting for Web pages to load. Time that could be spent doing the things we actually enjoy. To top it all off, when our computer breaks down, it's not like all that time learning how to use it pays off. We still have to call an expert to fix it. Or worse, go out and buy a new one. That's progress?

It might not seem like it at first, but your GPS receiver is a lot less complicated than your home computer and it's much easier to use. Best of all, your GPS receiver is designed to enhance the outdoor activities you enjoy most, not replace them. For this reason alone learning to use one is a lot more fun than tapping away at a computer keyboard. The better you are with your GPS receiver, the more time you're going to spend outside doing the things you love most, whether it's hiking or biking, fishing or hunting, or driving along scenic back roads in your car.

Here are some common questions first-time users ask about GPS:

Do I really have to read another manual?

Not at all. This book is not a manual. It's not a buyer's guide that will be outdated in a week. It's not even a guidebook in the traditional sense of the term. This book is a time machine. It will save you the time—and aggravation—it takes to become an expert with your GPS receiver. As nifty as they are, GPS receivers are merely a means to an end. This book is designed to move you along the GPS learning curve without getting bogged down in needless information, or getting fooled by the pitfalls that accompany every shiny new technology.

Maybe you already own a GPS receiver, but it's been collecting dust on a shelf ever since you took it out in the field and it didn't do what the salesman said it was going to do. Maybe you're thinking about buying one but aren't sure whether it'll work the way you want it to. In either case, you're doing the right thing in reading this book. You're getting educated. You certainly don't want to use your GPS receiver for the very first time on your vacation, or on the first day of deer season. If you do, I can guarantee you that your GPS receiver will end up at the bottom of your backpack or cargo pocket, or left underneath the spare tire in the trunk of your car.

You shouldn't have to spend your free time reading reams of high-tech jargon to learn how to use your GPS to its fullest advantage. This book is a jargon-free zone. Go ahead, flip through the pages. Take it for a spin. You won't find any mind-numbing phrases such as "radio signal propagation through the ionosphere." You won't be forced to wade through a lot of pointless background information for every nugget of solid advice. This book is about becoming a better driver, not a mechanic. By the time you reach the end of it you'll be confidently proficient at operating your GPS receiver. You'll understand how it works. And you'll get the most out of it, no matter what you do, where you go, or how you get there.

What the heck is GPS?

GPS stands for Global Positioning System. If I had a nickel for every time I heard the word "satellite" substituted for "system" I'd have enough money to buy a ranch in Montana. Am I a geek for getting annoyed at such a harmless mistake? Probably. But the difference is an important one to understand. When we say "GPS" we're talking about an entire $10 billion system, not a single, measly satellite. The system consists of 24 satellites that transmit radio signals to earth. Your GPS receiver, which picks up these signals and calculates them to figure out where you are, is a small yet critical part of this system. So what? It's a system, then. Big deal. Well, once you understand how the system works, which is explained in the first chapter, then you'll be much better at diagnosing potential problems and finding solutions rather than shaking your fist at the sky or tossing your GPS receiver in a drawer next to the broken TV remote.

What can this fancy "system" do for me?

The answer is as simple as it is revolutionary: The Global Positioning System can tell you where you are, where you've been and where you're going—within 15 meters (49 feet) 95% of the time. And it can do it anywhere in the world, at any time of day or night, in any weather. No other technology in the world can do this. Think about that for a moment. Getting safely from one place to another in a reasonable amount of time is one of the oldest, most important activities in all of human history, and up until now it's been one big gamble.

The combination of compass and map has worked fine for the past few hundred years, but a compass can't tell you where you've been. It also can't tell you precisely where you are in relation to what's around you. On the other hand, a map and compass are pretty good at indicating the direction you should be headed, something a GPS receiver can do in its sleep. GPS truly is a revolution in the history of navigation.

Don't get me wrong; a GPS receiver has limitations. It doesn't replace the map and compass, not until they invent batteries that live forever. But a GPS receiver's advantages far outweigh its shortcomings. No doubt about it. A GPS receiver takes the mystery—and danger—out of finding your way back to the boat ramp in a thick fog. Try that with a map and compass. It points you in the right direction when you're hungry and tired and night is falling and there's a fork in the trail that's not on the map. It shows you exactly where you saw that big buck last month when you were scouting ahead for bowhunting season. It gets you to the church on time and shows you where to fill up on gas, which is important because your best friend only gets married once. Sometimes twice, but your GPS receiver will come in handy then, too....

GPS is here to stay.

What will I learn by reading this book?

Exactly what you need to know. Nothing more, nothing less. But the best way to learn anything is to just get out there and do it. I highly recommend reading this book in sections and returning to it when you have a specific question or are ready to go to the next step.

CHAPTER 1

How GPS Works

Why should you care how the Global Positioning System works—as long as it works, right? Right. But how many technologies work perfectly 100% of the time, under all conditions? Not a single one. And that's fine if we're talking about a toaster or a fax machine. Besides a little inconvenience, your safety isn't an issue if they don't work as expected.

GPS, however, is categorically different. Sure, most of the time the loss of satellite signals isn't going to be the end of the world. But it only takes one unfortunate accident during a trip into unfamiliar wilderness, a first-time outing on a new lake or a wrong turn into a creepy neighborhood. Suddenly, understanding how your GPS receiver works—not merely how to press the buttons—becomes absolutely critical. Isn't that why we carry GPS receivers in the first place? As a safeguard against the unknown?

With a basic knowledge of how the system works, including its limitations, you won't be unpleasantly surprised in the field. To illustrate the key concepts behind GPS, I included a few simple exercises that you can try, just to see how these concepts work in reality. They won't take long to accomplish. Even if you're not a GPS beginner, I highly recommend doing the exercises because not many people take the few minutes necessary to understand what's going on inside the black box they rely on.

A Constellation of Satellites

For thousands of years people have looked to individual stars, constellations and planets to orient themselves on earth. As long as they didn't have to work on Monday morning, this system worked pretty well because navigating by stars, constellations and planets takes a lot of time. The way it works is simple. Heavenly bodies appear to travel in predictable paths across the sky. With certain tools—sextant, astrolabe, chronometer—experienced navigators could measure relative angles and distances between themselves and these reference points, giving them a fairly good idea of where they were on earth. Some navigators were so skilled that their measurements are still recorded on sea charts used every day in modern vessels crammed with sophisticated electronics.

The network of GPS satellites functions much like a constellation of stars. They move in predictable paths across the sky. You can't see them to navigate by, so they transmit radio signals that your GPS receiver picks up and uses as reference points to calculate its position on earth. The system is nothing short of miraculous when you consider how it works and what it can do.

The system consists of 24 satellites, often referred to as a constellation, that are orbiting 11,000 miles (18,000 km) above the earth twice a day. That means at any given time it's theoretically possible for your GPS receiver to get signals from 12 satellites. The other 12 are on the other side of the earth. However, among the 12 available satellites, some will be so low on the horizon that the curvature of the earth will block the signal. But that's okay, because as we'll learn later in this chapter, you only need four satellites to navigate.

The big advantage that GPS has over celestial navigation

techniques used by ancient mariners is its availability. Stars are only visible on clear nights, whereas GPS satellite signals are available 24 hours a day, in any weather. That means your GPS receiver will work anywhere in the world at any time of day. Instant, highly accurate position information at the touch of a button. Like I said, revolutionary. Better still, a GPS receiver is much easier to fit in your pocket than a sextant.

Initializing Your GPS Receiver

Your GPS has traveled hundreds or thousands of miles before it ended up on a store shelf, where it sat for a few months before you took it home. It's confused and has no idea where it is. To get it familiar with its surroundings, you need to "initialize" it. It may also require re-initialization if it's been turned off for a long time or has traveled over 300 miles since the last time you used it. Of course, you don't *have to* initialize your GPS receiver. You can simply turn it on and let it figure out where it is all on its own. In that case, it may take twenty minutes to initialize, usually much less, to be ready for navigating.

An Exercise to Initialize

To initialize your GPS receiver, take it outside where you have a clear view of the sky and turn it on.

After accepting the legal warnings, you'll be asked to specify where you are. This usually requires little more than choosing a continent, and then a specific region or state, from a map or menu.

Using the rocker keypad, point to your approximate location and press ENTER

After you've accomplished this simple task, the satellite status page will pop up. From here you can watch the GPS receiver track satellites as they come in and out of view. Status bars show the strength of each satellite signal. What you can't see is your GPS receiver memorizing the satellite almanac, which is basically a calendar that forecasts where each satellite is going to be at a particular time in this general area.

The next time you turn on your GPS receiver it will flip through this almanac and lock on much quicker, since it already knows where in the sky to look for satellites. Now go back inside your house before your neighbors mistake you for a refugee from a Star Trek convention.

Limitations to GPS Navigation

As revolutionary as it is, the Global Positioning System has a few drawbacks. Once you're aware of these limitations and know how to work around them, they won't seriously affect where, when and how you use your GPS receiver.

Blocking the View

The biggest limiting factor is the nature of the radio signal transmitted by GPS satellites. It can't penetrate solid objects, so forget about using GPS inside structures. It's possible to receive signals when standing next to a big window, but as the satellites zip around the earth, these signals won't last long.

GPS receivers might also have difficulty locking onto satellite signals under dense tree coverage, or when you're navigating in a steep ravine, canyon, a city with many tall buildings, inside a car and so on. Even your body can block or "shade" GPS signals!

Under some of these conditions your GPS receiver won't work at all, or it'll work so intermittently that you'll be too annoyed to bother with it.

Does that mean you'll be forced to operate your GPS receiver only in the open desert or high on a windy mountaintop? Of course not. There are often many more satellites in view than are necessary to navigate safely. It's not uncommon to have seven or eight satellites vying for your receiver's attention. The system was designed so at least four satellites will be in view at any one time anywhere on the planet. If a signal becomes blocked, your GPS receiver will jump to a better signal.

An external antenna helps immensely in conditions where signals are being blocked, especially when driving. In other situations, however, you might have to find a clearing in the foliage to get a view of the sky wide enough for a position fix. Signal blockage is not an issue on open water or when flying.

Flying with the Crows

When navigating with a GPS receiver, it's important to understand that it can't see what's between you and the place you're

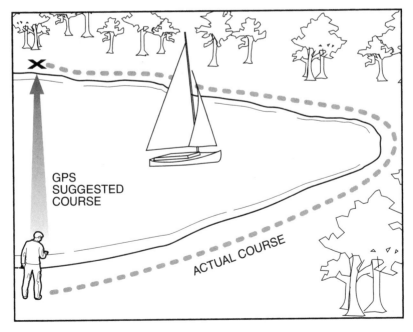

GPS
SUGGESTED
COURSE

ACTUAL COURSE

headed. All that wonderful information it gives you is based on straight-line navigation. Why should you care? If there's a sandbar or a swamp or a traffic jam between you and your destination, your GPS receiver doesn't care. It's determined to get you where you're going on the shortest route possible. It'll tell you that your destination is only 1 mile (1.6 km) away "as the crow flies" when, in reality, getting around that obstacle is going to take you 5 miles (8 km) off course.

For this reason alone, it's a good idea not to throw away your maps and compass; in fact, as you will see later on, when used together, the trinity of map, compass and GPS receiver can be very powerful.

Vertically Challenged

Your GPS receiver is very good at figuring out horizontal coordinates—that is, latitude and longitude—but it's not quite as good at figuring out elevation. The reason has more to do with the limits of geometry than some inherent flaw of the system itself. The only thing you need to remember is that elevation readings are generally 50% less accurate than your horizontal readings. Therefore, if your GPS receiver estimates your position error (EPE, or "estimated position error") at 10 meters (33 feet), your elevation reading may be off by 15 meters (49 feet). If knowing your exact elevation is critical to your recreational activity, you might want to consider buying a GPS receiver with a built-in altimeter that separately measures barometric pressure for accurate elevation readings.

Keep It Moving

Every single bit of information your receiver displays is based on one simple mathematical formula that we all learned in grade school: Distance = Velocity x Time. The formula can be rearranged to figure out the other variables involved:

$$Velocity = Distance \div Time$$

$$Time = Distance \div Velocity$$

It's the same formula you used to solve those wicked word problems that always seemed to involve a car, traveling at 40 mph (65 kmph), on a collision course with a freight train, traveling at 60 mph (97 kmph). The car and the train were blissfully unaware that 20 miles (32 km) separated them at the moment. Your job in math class was to figure out precisely when the carnage was going to occur based on these variables.

The trouble is, take away any one of these variables and you don't have a formula. Without a formula, you can't calculate anything. Your GPS receiver needs movement—velocity, or speed—in order to tell you what direction you're headed in, how far away your destination is and how long it's going to take to get there.

Does that mean you have to keep moving every time you want to get an accurate position reading? No. Your GPS receiver will always give you a reading, no matter what you're doing.

Battery Dependence

Unfortunately, electrical power sources aren't available in most places you'll want to take your GPS receiver. Rechargeable batteries might just as well be regular alkalines in that case.

No matter what, all batteries are doomed to die eventually. GPS receivers are also subject to malfunction like any other electronic gadget. It can "crash" for reasons known only to the little silicon elves that live inside the plastic case.

GPS receivers, like cell phones and other electronic gadgets, have a backlit screen to make it easier to see in dim light. Press a key and the backlight comes on, whether it's high noon or the dead of night. Nothing chews up battery life faster than backlighting, however. It's a good idea to switch it off permanently in the setup menu, and turn it on only when you know you'll be using your GPS receiver to navigate at night, while driving for example. Or when navigating to a duck blind at dawn.

The point is, once the screen goes blank, whether the cause is dead batteries or a fried chipboard, the unit is utterly useless. You can't even burn it for warmth. So always remember to carry extra batteries!

An Exercise to Reveal Vulnerabilities

GPS receivers are like four-year-old children—they need to keep moving in order to make sense of anything. And the only way to stop them is with a wall or some other solid, stationary object. In this simple exercise we'll demonstrate two of your GPS receiver's biggest limitations: its reliance on movement to indicate direction, and its vulnerability to "shading" or satellite signal blockage.

Now that your GPS receiver is initialized and comfortable with your neighborhood, go outside and power it up. If it has a clear view of the sky, it should take less than a minute to achieve a position fix.

Once it's locked on to enough satellite signals, find the screen displaying a compass rose (it looks like the dial on a standard compass, with indicators for north, south, east and west) and go for a stroll around the block. Notice how the compass rose rotates as you make changes in direction? If you turn east, the top of the compass rose swivels toward the big E, and so on.

Now go back home and stand in your yard facing north, or any direction that you know for certain. Turn around slowly without moving off your spot. Notice how the compass rose or needle doesn't move?

Return to the same position you started in, facing the direction you know for certain (let's say it's north for example's sake). Is there a big N floating at the top of the compass rose? Probably not. It's probably pointing in the direction that you were headed before you stopped. Without movement—velocity or speed—your GPS receiver can't make sense of the world.

The digital compass rose might look like a real compass, but it's not.

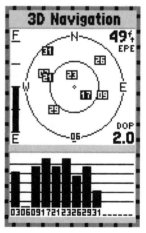

This satellite status page is taking readings from 8 satellites.

15

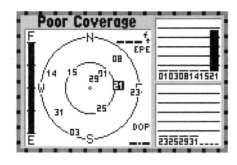

This unit is getting information from only 1 satellite.

Before you head back inside, find the satellite status page, the one with the bar graphs on it. Count the number of solid bars—that's how many satellite signals your GPS receiver is locked onto. They may be shifting up and down as satellites zoom through space far above your head, their signals getting stronger and weaker.

Now walk to the front of your house, or to the side, it doesn't matter, as long as you can safely keep your eye on the satellite status page while walking. Keep going until you're at the front door or you bump into the wall.

You should see a drop-off of some of the satellite signals, indicated by a few status bars suddenly getting short or disappearing altogether from the screen. What the heck happened? As you walked you slowly changed the angle at which satellite signals could get to your GPS receiver without running into your house. The closer you got, the steeper the angle, until pretty much any satellite signal except those coming in directly overhead or from behind you were blocked by a wall.

You deliberately "shaded" your GPS receiver, something that will happen occasionally the more places you take it. At least now you won't panic when the "Poor GPS Coverage" window pops up on your screen.

Let's Talk Satellites

Besides the bustling activity of little silicon elves, what exactly is going on inside your GPS receiver? How does it turn satellite signals into measurements of latitude and longitude? It all comes down to geometry, for without it your GPS receiver is just a radio that doesn't play music.

The signal broadcast by GPS satellites is encoded with all kinds of information that can effectively be boiled down to "Hey, my name is Satellite 04, I'm over here and this is the time." That's what it's shouting to your GPS receiver at regular intervals, like a broken record. If two more satellites come into range shouting the same information—but specific to their particular positions and times—your GPS receiver can use the principle of triangulation to figure out where it is.

The Rule of Threes

Let's assume all three satellites are at different places in the sky, not an unreasonable assumption since the system was designed to keep many satellites zooming overhead in all directions. Your GPS receiver will "hear" each satellite shouting its name slightly differently because each message arrives at a slightly different time.

You know how this works if you've ever played that most famous of all swimming-pool games, Marco Polo. By shouting "Marco!" and evoking "Polo!" from all the other players, it's easy to tell who's closer and who's farther away. If you weren't so busy lunging at the other players and stood there for a few moments, you could figure out roughly where you were in the pool by using the technique of triangulation.

Let's say Joe sounds like he's 3 feet (1 m) away to the left. Diane sounds like she's 10 feet (3 m) away to the right. Sam sounds like he's 15 feet (4.5 m) behind you. Given this information, you figure out that you must be near the shallow end of the pool, just for this example. Depending on the "signals" from the other players, you could be at the deep end as well, or in the middle and so on.

Your GPS receiver works the same way. It uses triangulation by measuring the time differential between each satellite transmission it's tuned to and calculating the various distances.

Of the three satellites, let's say the first one is 11,000 miles (18,000 km) away. As far as your GPS receiver is concerned, your location could be at any point on the compass 11,000 miles away from the satellite. That's a big sphere, big enough to contain points floating around in the vacuum of space, some scattered in China and at least one that's the place where you're actually standing. Not very accurate, but in the ballpark if you're an astronaut.

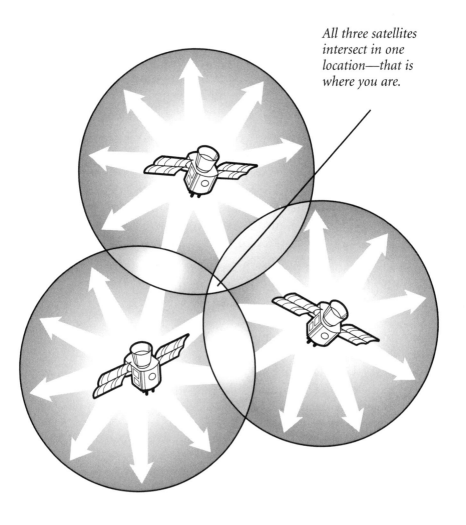

All three satellites intersect in one location—that is where you are.

Let's bring a second satellite into the equation. This satellite is calculated to be 12,000 miles (19,000 km) away from your GPS receiver, as represented on the illustration by the sphere of possible locations surrounding it. That's an even bigger area than the first satellite! What good is that?

Good question, but your GPS receiver is smart enough to know that it can only be located somewhere in the common area where the two spheres of possibility bump into each other. While that narrows the range of possibilities quite a bit, it's still a big area and not very precise information.

Enter the third GPS satellite, calculated to be 13,000 miles (21,000 km) from your GPS receiver. When you overlay its sphere of possible locations onto the other two spheres, suddenly it all becomes clear. There's only one place that all the spheres intersect (actually, there are two locations, but one of them is thrown out as an unreasonable possibility). That place of intersection is where you are.

The Right Address, Every Time

Your GPS receiver races through these mind-numbing calculations in a fraction of the time it takes to read this sentence. That makes it the most expensive calculator on the planet! The trick it performs with the numbers is the part most relevant to you. You see, every square inch (cm) of the earth has a unique address, including that patch of dirt beneath your feet. Your GPS receiver can remember the address of this exact spot no matter where you go. And you can return to it at any time, as long as you save it as a "waypoint"—sort of like telling the GPS receiver to write it down in an address book.

On your travels away from this address, your receiver continuously updates your position, many times per second. It can calculate speed and distance from this address, or heading (direction) and distance to wherever you're going. It also calculates the distance from your starting point and any other point you might have stored in its memory.

Basically, if a measurement has anything to do with time, distance, speed or location your GPS receiver can display it. All because it knows exactly where it is at any given time.

2D or Not To 3D

If your GPS receiver is locked on to signals from at least three satellites, this is called a two-dimensional (2D) or "horizontal" position fix. It gives you latitude and longitude coordinates, but not vertical elevation. Your GPS receiver needs to hear from at least four satellites to get latitude, longitude and elevation. This is called a three-dimensional (3D) fix.

Most of the time you'll be navigating in 3D mode, but as we now know, sometimes signals get blocked or a satellite drops over the horizon, putting your receiver into 2D mode. This is important to know if elevation is critical to your activity, such as mountain climbing, and also because a 2D fix is less accurate than a 3D fix.

How do you know when your GPS receiver has enough satellites in view? Any unit will tell you when there's poor coverage due to lack of good signals. A pop-up window will appear saying "Poor GPS Coverage" or something to this effect. Also, in the corner of the satellite status page, most receivers will indicate whether you're navigating in 3D or 2D mode. (We'll cover the different kinds of information displayed on each "page" or screen of a typical GPS receiver, and how to manipulate this information, in Chapter 3.)

A Note to Conspiracy Theorists

A GPS receiver is not a tracking device. By owning one, you are not allowing secret government agents, or anyone else, to track your movements from the hardware store to your shack in the woods where you live. I don't care what you've seen in the movies, a GPS receiver is, by definition, a receiver. Nothing more. It cannot transmit data on any radio frequency.

A device that sends and receives information on a radio frequency is called a transceiver. Some GPS manufacturers sell units that combine a walkie-talkie type of radio with a GPS receiver, making it possible to send and receive location information to and from similarly equipped units. But that's by choice of the user, and it still doesn't allow anyone to track your movements.

You may now safely remove the tinfoil from your head and take the blankets off the windows.

Using Your Trail

Owning a GPS receiver with a fresh set of batteries doesn't mean you can't get lost. I once heard a complaint from an old-time woodsman—I'll call him Crusty—that illustrates this point perfectly.

Crusty was suspicious of any technology more complicated than a jackknife. He claimed he could get around the woods by his sense of smell alone. One Christmas he got a GPS receiver from his children, who were worried about Crusty getting older and spending all that time in the woods by himself. What if he got disoriented and fell down and hurt himself? To humor his children, Crusty took the GPS with him on his rambles. Sometimes he even turned it on, only to turn it off again a few minutes later, grumbling the whole time. Pretty soon the fancy new GPS receiver was gathering dust on a shelf next to some old pinecones. There was talk among his children of putting Crusty in a home for cranky old-timers.

"That darn thing is no good. It only tells me where I am," Crusty groused one day while we were sitting on his front porch. "What good is that? I already know where I am!"

Crusty might not be the kind of guy you'd want fixing your TV or babysitting your children, but he's no fool. The fact is, Crusty was absolutely right. At its most basic level, a GPS receiver can only tell you where you are. That's what it does best. And it does it automatically without any input from you. If you get lost in the woods, stranded in a strange city or are drifting blindly on a foggy lake, your GPS receiver will rather unhelpfully tell you where you are. If you are lost, what good is knowing the latitude and longitude? That's not going to get you found. Not unless you have a VHF radio to call in your coordinates to a search-and-rescue agency such as the Coast Guard.

So, was Crusty right about his GPS receiver? Yes and no. He was right in theory, even though Crusty doesn't trust theories. Nor does he understand them. But you do. If a GPS receiver is capable of figuring out where it is at any given moment, then having a permanent reference point—or two, or three, or 153—stored in its memory will make navigation a whole lot easier. That way, wherever you go, you'll always know where you are in relation to that saved location(s). But how do those locations get in your GPS receiver?

Don't Eat the Breadcrumbs

Most people know the fable of Hansel and Gretel. If you don't, here's the short version: Lost and harassed by a hungry witch, this brother and sister eventually find their way out of the dark woods thanks to a trail of breadcrumbs they'd dropped earlier on their way in. The end. For our purposes, the important part of this story is the breadcrumbs. Your GPS receiver performs the same clever tactic pioneered by Hansel and Gretel by automatically dropping electronic "breadcrumbs" wherever you go from the moment you turn it on.

The simplest thing a GPS receiver can do for you is trace your exact path to your current position by dropping digital "bread-crumbs" all the way.

This electronic breadcrumb trail is called a "track log." The individual crumbs are called "track log points," "track points" or just "points." The track log can be navigated in the same exact manner in which Hansel and Gretel navigated their way out of the dark forest—by retracing their steps.

If our cantankerous old friend Crusty had the patience to turn on his GPS and consult it now and then as he strolled through the woods, he would've seen a dotted line connecting his present position with his point of departure in the backyard of his log cabin. That line would've shown every turn he made to avoid fallen tree limbs, streams and other obstacles, making it a cinch for him to avoid these same obstacles on the way back home—all without ever pressing a single button except to turn on the unit. (You'll find out more about navigating a track log in Chapter 5.)

Waypoints

Another way for your GPS receiver to remember specific locations is to plug them in yourself. This requires a little more direct collaboration between you and your receiver than navigating a track log. Most receivers make it easy to save waypoints, which are simply significant locations to which you may later want to return, such as a campsite, a great hole-in-the-wall restaurant that you stumbled upon one evening or a productive fishing hole. They may be significant ground features that rarely change from year to year (trailheads, river crossings, shoals) or temporary yet important locations (seasonal tree stands, the place you parked the truck, good place to gather dry wood). There's no limit to what you can make into a waypoint.

Usually it takes just one press of a button to create a waypoint and assign it a unique electronic address, after which your GPS receiver will give you the option to name it. Even if you go halfway around the world, you'll always know exactly how far away you are from every waypoint in the unit's memory, and the direction you need to travel to get to any of them—as the crow flies, of course.

At a glance, you can see waypoints in relation to each other, or locate the same coordinates on a map to make trip planning easier. You can share waypoints with a friend's GPS receiver, either by punching in the coordinates manually or digitally downloading them into the other receiver's memory.

Exercise to Give "Home" a Name

I've heard many stories about people losing their GPS receivers, only to have them returned by kind strangers. How did they know where to return it? Because not only were they honest, but smart, too. They looked at the list of waypoints saved in the unit's memory, found the one labeled "Home," and corresponding latitude and longitude coordinates with a street address—this can be done on the Web, or with special software, or simply by using the receiver itself to navigate.

Take your GPS outside and power it up. You should be familiar with the whole initialization process now. Once it's locked on, press the "Mark" or "Enter" button. A window will pop up that

Your first waypoint should always be your original address; that way you will always know how to get home.

looks disturbingly like those forms you're always being asked to fill out on the Internet. Your GPS receiver will give you the default option to name this waypoint "wypt01," or something equally uninspired.

Highlight the name box and hit the Enter key to rename the way-point "Home." Get into the habit right away of taking the time to name waypoints, or you never will.

If your GPS receiver has a posi-tion-averaging function and asks if you'd like to activate it, highlight "yes" and hit Enter. This won't take long. Position averaging means that the receiver is taking hundreds of sample position fixes and aver-aging them all together to arrive at a fix more precise than a single roll of the dice, which is what you did when you pressed the "Mark" key.

Now all you have to do is hit "Save" and you're done! Now, wherever you go, you will always know which way is home, even if you don't ever want to go back there.

Basemaps

There's a good chance that your GPS receiver comes with a basemap already loaded into its memory. Typically, such basemaps include fixed features that aren't likely to change much: rivers and lakes, cities and towns, highways and state roads, airports, state borders and so on. As you move, these fea-tures also move in relation to your position, making navigation a snap.

While basemaps make it very convenient to navigate to most places that you might find on a road map, they don't show the kind of information a hiker might need to get around the backcountry, or for someone trying to find a specific street address in a strange city for the first time. You'll need to supplement the built-in basemap with additional, downloadable maps for more specific uses, such as topographic maps for hikers and hunters, sea charts for anglers, or city street maps for the road tripper.

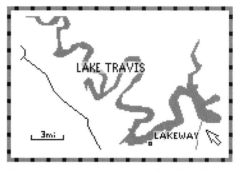

Basemaps are quite general and only give you the basics for navigating.

Crusty's GPS receiver has a built-in basemap, but there's a big blank space on the map page where Crusty knows his beloved woods to be. Some map! That only confirmed for him that his children were wasting their money on useless junk.

What Crusty didn't take the time to realize was that his GPS receiver's built-in basemap did show the county road that formed the northern border of his property, even if it didn't give much information about the property itself. As he rambled aimlessly through the woods, he might've seen how his course was taking him straight north toward the county road and an unfortunate date with an out-of-control logging truck barreling around the corner.

What's the lesson here? Don't end up like Crusty, alone in a home for cranky old-timers. Wait—you didn't think Crusty got hit by that logging truck, did you? You should be ashamed! No, for the purposes of this book, we need Crusty to hang around a little while longer….

CHAPTER 2

GPS Accuracy, WAAS and DGPS

This is what it's all about—accuracy. Everyone has heard stories, both good and bad, about the accuracy of GPS receivers. Back in the days when 100 meters (328 feet) of error was common, I had a buddy who insisted that his GPS receiver got him to the foot of his tree stand on the opening day of deer season, in the dark, every year. Then there's the guy who claimed that his GPS pointed him in the wrong direction and actually got him lost while hunting elk in another state.

Both stories are equally doubtful. This chapter will help you separate fact from fiction when it comes to the accuracy of your GPS receiver, how correction systems like WAAS and DGPS work and the conditions under which the whole thing won't work as well as you expect—or need—it to work.

Selective Availability (SA)

Few technologies as groundbreaking as GPS have been the subject of so many rumors and myths about their performance. The biggest source of myth has to do with something called Selective Availability (SA), which is a fancy term for the U.S. military's old policy of degrading the accuracy of the civilian GPS signal. The idea was to keep GPS from being used with any precision by potential enemies—and subsequently, by the people who paid for the system in the first place, you and me.

SA was turned off in May 2000. The military found another way to degrade the GPS signal on a limited regional basis—over Iraq, for example—instead of ruining the whole thing for everybody in the world. But when SA was active GPS receivers could be off the mark by more than 300 feet (91 m)!

Many people bought GPS receivers and tried them out for the first time in their backyards. Why not, right? It's a natural thing to do. These people would mark a waypoint at the edge of the yard, near a picnic table for example. Then they'd try to return to the picnic table in a sort of home experiment with accuracy. Of course, their GPS receiver failed miserably under these conditions. Not too many backyards are more than 300 feet square.

So, those brave GPS pioneers would be wandering around aimlessly, while their GPS receivers pointed in all directions but the picnic table. Why? Because they were operating well within the 300-foot circle of error caused by SA. Many people ended up disappointed and gave up on GPS. If this expensive new gadget couldn't navigate with any accuracy in their own backyards, it certainly wasn't going to work any better in the woods.

And they were partly right. Not because GPS was a bad technology. But because of Selective Availability.

A Little History

SA can't be blamed for the difficulties many people experienced in the early days of GPS, however. User-friendly mapping units that we take for granted today were years away from being marketed. And using a GPS receiver in your car was impossible, unless you were a geek with an extra roll of duct tape and an external antenna. The user interface on most GPS receivers—what you actually saw on the display—was a crude jumble of numbers with few graphics and confusing sub-menus. In short, GPS receivers were inaccurate and not very easy to operate.

Some years ago, while SA was still active, there was no such thing as a correction system to improve accuracy. You had to get by on the standard, error-ridden GPS signal.

Units with 12-parallel-channel receivers were just coming onto the market and they were expensive. Single-channel receivers were the norm. And they were practically useless for any serious outdoor activity that didn't take place on the open plains or on the water. Just walking under a tree would often cause single-channel receivers to lose GPS coverage entirely.

Early GPS manufacturers didn't help matters. They marketed their gadgets with deceptive language about accuracy and ability to hold on to satellite signals under certain conditions. For instance, they often claimed that their single-channel GPS receiver "tracks up to 12 satellites." Well, if you didn't know any better, wouldn't you think this was a 12-channel receiver? Just because a GPS receiver "tracks" 12 satellites, however, doesn't mean it's a 12-parallel-channel receiver. A lot of people didn't realize they'd actually bought a single-channel receiver until they took it into the woods and lost all satellite coverage. Yikes!

Error Adjustment

The Global Positioning System isn't quite perfect because, for one thing, the earth itself isn't perfect. Now we have ways of compensating for errors in GPS readings that cause a loss of accuracy.

But before we talk about correction systems, we need to understand what they were designed to correct. In a perfect world satellite signals would beam straight to your GPS receiver with no interference whatsoever. But in our world, signals bounce off buildings, bedrock and other flat, hard surfaces, messing up their timing. This is called "multipath error."

Another source of error in the GPS signal comes from the earth's atmosphere. Constant shifts in the thickness of the ionosphere caused by solar storms distort satellite signals by slowing them down as they pass through.

And what would an expensive chunk of electronics flying through space be if it didn't occasionally break down or stray from its orbital path? This type of inaccuracy is called "ephemeris error."

Ultra-precise timing is essential to GPS accuracy. To accomplish this, engineers install atomic clocks aboard each GPS satellite that are so accurate they lose only one second every million years or so. But the clock in your GPS receiver isn't nearly as precise—or as heavy and costly. The difference between your receiver's time and the satellite's time is called "clock error." You have to give up a little accuracy in your GPS receiver to get portability and a price that wouldn't bankrupt a small country—or make you radioactive.

You might be asking how the U.S. military gets pinpoint accuracy. Or for that matter, how do land surveyors mark property lines and bulldozers grade roadbeds with accuracy that can be measured in millimeters? If they can get that kind of accuracy,

Here's a breakdown of exactly where the term of 15-meter (49-ft) accuracy comes from:

ERROR SOURCE	LOSS OF ACCURACY
Multipath	1.5 m (5 ft)
Atmospheric	
Ionosphere	7 m (23 ft)
Troposphere	1 m (3 ft)
Clock and Ephemeris	4 m (13 ft)
Receiver Noise	1.5 m (5 ft)
Total	**15 m (49 ft)**

why can't you? The first one is easy. The military has its own special GPS signal that civilians can't use. As for land surveyors and other high-end GPS users, they lug around suitcases full of expensive equipment that helps them get around the standard sources of error.

Considering the unavoidable limitations, it's amazing your GPS receiver can regularly achieve 15-meter (49-feet) accuracy, and frequently do better than that. While correction signals such as the Wide Area Augmentation System (WAAS) and Differential GPS (DGPS) can't totally eliminate natural sources of error, they can get you within spitting distance of your destination.

Examples of Error

Handheld GPS receivers are subject to unavoidable sources of error, including:

• *Intentional:* In the past, the U.S. military degraded the GPS signal, limiting accuracy to 100 meters (109 yards). This was called Selective Availability (SA). Since 2000, the military set SA to zero and has no plans to use it again.

• *Atmospheric delay:* Satellite signals slow down as they pass through the earth's atmosphere.

• *Ephemeris:* Wobbly satellites inaccurately report their location.

• *Clock:* The clock in your GPS receiver isn't nearly as accurate as the atomic clocks used by GPS satellites, creating timing errors.

• *Multipath:* Satellite signals bounce off solid objects such as buildings or rock faces before reaching your receiver.

• *Available satellites:* There will be times when your GPS receiver can't "see" enough satellite signals to calculate an accurate position. Buildings, canyon walls and dense foliage can block signals, which reduces accuracy or causes your receiver to quit displaying any position reading, at least temporarily.

• *Satellite geometry:* Even if you're locked on to enough satellites for a position fix, the satellites may be clustered in the same part of the sky, reducing accuracy.

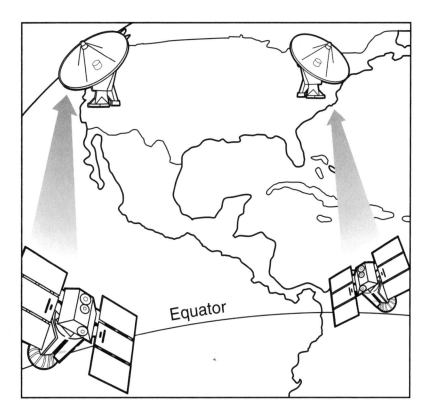

Equator

Wide Area Augmentation System (WAAS)

The first users of the Global Positioning System were pilots. It's easy to see why. In the air, there are no landmarks, especially in the clouds when the ground isn't visible. There's no such thing as a minor accident in the air. Both commercial and civil aviators are required to fly along strict routes to avoid smashing into each other, or into the sides of mountains. GPS is great at helping pilots stay on course from airport to airport. But since GPS vertical or altitude readings are generally 50% less accurate than horizontal positioning, the system isn't very good for the most dangerous parts of any flight: takeoff and landing.

In the late 1990s, the Federal Aviation Administration (FAA) began developing a system to boost GPS accuracy for pilots called the Wide Area Augmentation System (WAAS). It's still under development, but the system was approved for use on land in 2000.

So what is it? WAAS is a network of land-based stations that double-checks the standard GPS signal for errors, like atmospheric delays and temporary satellite outages. These ground stations make a correction to the signal then relay it to special WAAS satellites in stationary orbit above the equator (they are in the same place at all times relative to the earth, unlike regular GPS satellites). The two WAAS satellites—one over the Atlantic Ocean, another over the Pacific—broadcast the correction signal to WAAS-enabled GPS receivers.

WAAS Advantages

The great thing about a WAAS-enabled GPS receiver is that it can get you to within 10 to 16 feet (3 to 5 m) of your destination. That's five times more accurate than a standard GPS receiver! Those numbers are good, but not good enough for landing an airplane on a runway, where every inch (cm) of altitude is absolutely critical. For that reason pilots have a variety of other navigation systems to help them.

The other big advantage is that WAAS signals are broadcast on the same frequency as regular GPS signals. That means no additional hardware or antennas are required for your GPS receiver to process the signal. Just turn it on and go. You gain extra accuracy without losing the portability and convenience of an ordinary handheld GPS receiver.

WAAS Limitations

There are a few important limitations to WAAS that the salesperson might not have mentioned. Since the WAAS correction signal is broadcast on the same frequency as the regular GPS signal, it works by line-of-sight. That means it can be blocked by mountains, steep ravines and canyons—all the things that can block a regular GPS signal.

However, WAAS signals are even more vulnerable to blockage compared to the regular GPS signal. Why? Aren't they the same? Not exactly.

The frequency is the same, but WAAS satellites sit in one place relatively low above the horizon, exactly the opposite of high-orbiting GPS satellites. This is fine for airplanes flying high above terrain, or for boaters on open water where there's nothing to block a signal skimming in low over the earth.

For navigating on land, it's a different story. That means if you are fishing a reservoir surrounded by tall ridges, the WAAS signal may be blocked by hills. Or if you're bushwhacking in dense foliage, the WAAS signal may not be available at all.

Unlike the 24 regular GPS satellites zooming all over the sky, there are only two WAAS satellites and they don't move from their fixed positions. If you lose the WAAS signal, another one isn't going to come into view a few minutes later. When it's gone, it's gone until you move to a place where the signal becomes available again.

Because WAAS satellites are fixed in place, above the equator, the farther north you go in the United States the lower the satellites get to the horizon until the curvature of the earth blocks them completely. The FAA is looking into this limitation and has plans to launch a third WAAS satellite to improve spotty coverage, but a date hasn't been set.

The important thing to understand is that, despite these limitations, your WAAS-enabled GPS receiver will still work fine without the WAAS signal. It just won't benefit from the additional accuracy WAAS provides when the signal is blocked.

Differential GPS (DGPS)

Before WAAS there was DGPS, which is good for 3 to 10 feet (1 to 3 m) of accuracy. Both systems increase the accuracy of your GPS receiver by counteracting the natural errors that occur in satellite signals. Both systems consist of a network of ground stations. But the similarity ends there.

Where WAAS was designed for pilots, DGPS applies almost exclusively to offshore boaters and fishermen. DGPS correction signals are broadcast from land-based beacons, not satellites. These beacons know exactly where they are. They are found only on the coasts, in addition to shorelines of major bodies of water, such as the Great Lakes and the Mississippi River basin. They check their known location against the GPS signal and calculate the difference between the two. After adjusting for the "differential," the beacon broadcasts a correction message to GPS receivers in the area capable of receiving it.

DGPS Advantages

On open water there are no landmarks. A 3- to 10-foot (1- to 3-m) accuracy, then, is critical for marine applications. Imagine an oil tanker navigating through a narrow channel surrounded by shoals and rocks, or commercial vessels trying to negotiate through a tricky port with a lot of other ships. Or in our case, an angler looking for that secret hole where the big fish hang out. Regular GPS will get you in the right place, but it won't put you right on top of—or keep you away from—any bottom structure.

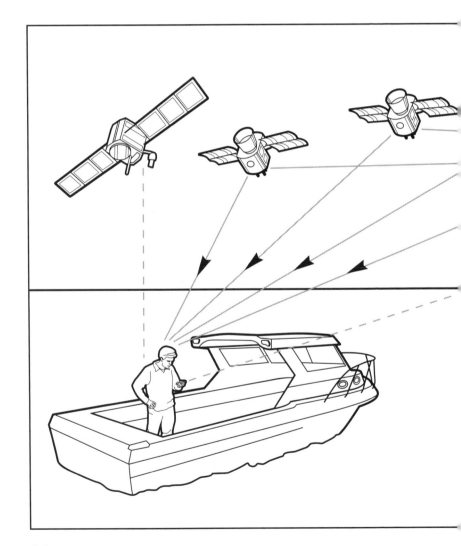

DGPS signals aren't broadcast on the GPS frequency. They have their own dedicated frequency that hugs the earth and wraps around obstacles that might otherwise block a WAAS or regular GPS signal. This makes the system ideal for navigating in busy harbors where loss of the signal due to blockage could mean disaster (See illustration on page 36).

There are 75 DGPS locations nationwide, and more being added. All of them are managed by the U.S. Coast Guard. The DGPS system is a proven technology that's been around for more than a decade, and will be here for many decades to come.

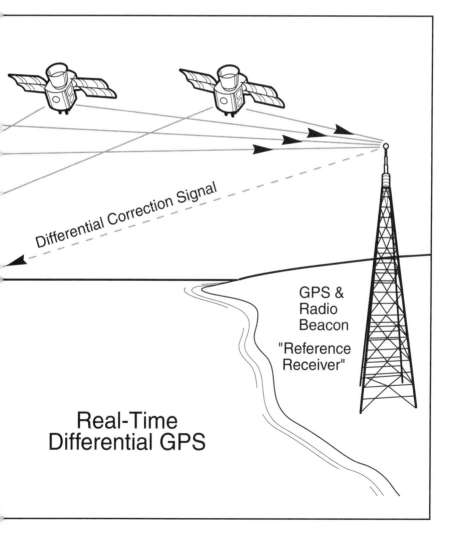

Differential Correction Signal

GPS &
Radio
Beacon

"Reference
Receiver"

**Real-Time
Differential GPS**

DGPS Limitations

Like anything that seems too good to be true, DGPS does have some important limitations. Hunters and hikers can't use it because DGPS signals are confined mainly to coastal areas. If you're hunting elk in Montana or hiking in New Hampshire the nearest DGPS beacon is probably several hundred miles away.

What if you're fishing one of Minnesota's thousands of lakes? If DGPS was designed for mariners, you'd have a better chance as a freshwater fisherman, right? Not necessarily. In most cases, inland lakes and waterways aren't served by DGPS. There just isn't enough commercial traffic to justify the expense of maintaining DGPS beacons in out-of-the-way areas.

If you want to take advantage of DGPS, check with the Coast Guard to see if there are any DGPS beacons near you.

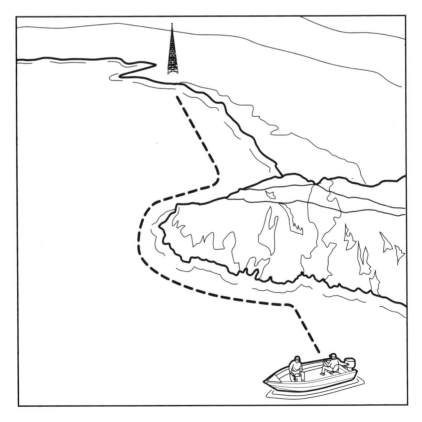

Even if you could get a DGPS correction in your favorite hunting grounds, you still probably wouldn't want to lug around the extra equipment necessary to receive the signal. Unlike WAAS-enabled receivers, DGPS requires the use of a separate antenna to receive the DGPS correction and a cable to attach the antenna to the GPS receiver. Dragging a cable and a beacon receiver and your GPS receiver through a briar patch is nobody's idea of a good time.

For the price of all the extras alone, you could buy a WAAS-enabled GPS receiver. DGPS is really designed to work like most marine electronics—fixed permanently to a console.

Satellite Geometry and Accuracy

There's one source of error that you *can* do something about, even if it just means waiting around for fifteen minutes until it passes. This kind of error has nothing to do with atomic clocks or wobbly satellite orbits or the thickness of the ionosphere.

In Chapter 1, we learned how a GPS receiver determines its position on earth by triangulation. To get the best possible accuracy, the receiver needs four satellites spread out over the sky. Why does it matter where the satellites are if all you need is four good signals? It all has to do with geometry.

In the field, poor satellite geometry can cost you hundreds of feet (meters) of position error.

Let's go back to the example we used to explain triangulation: You're back in the pool playing Marco Polo. You shout, "Marco!" The other players shout, "Polo!" By the sound of it they're all around you. If you use the other players as reference points (to the left and to the right, in front and behind), and their shouts of "Polo!" as signals broadcast from those points (some close, some far away), you can figure out roughly where you are in the pool. This is good geometry.

Now let's rearrange the other players to simulate bad geometry. Instead of being spread out at different points in the pool, imagine if they were treading water around the same spot. Suddenly it's not so easy to triangulate because all the shouts are apparently emanating from the same reference point.

It works the same way with GPS constellations. If the satellites

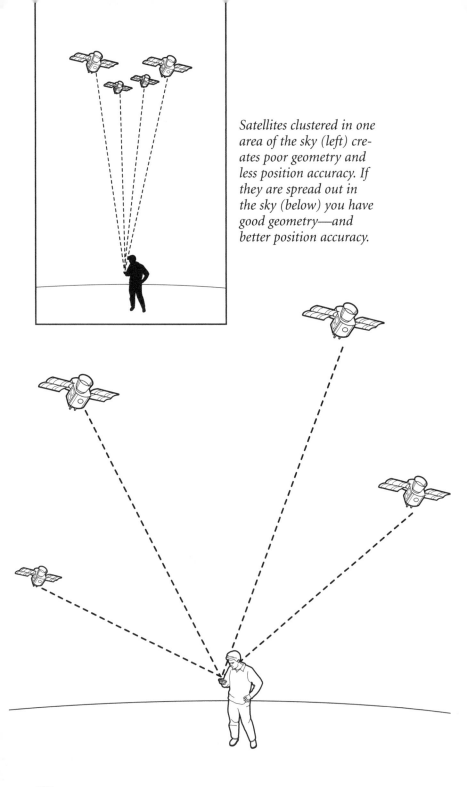

Satellites clustered in one area of the sky (left) creates poor geometry and less position accuracy. If they are spread out in the sky (below) you have good geometry—and better position accuracy.

are spread out across the sky, you're going to get a more accurate position reading than you would from four satellites clustered in the same part of the sky.

The good thing is that GPS receivers are smart enough to analyze the angles of all the satellites in view and choose the four that give the best geometry. Now and then, especially when some signals are being blocked and only a few are available, it's difficult getting four satellites spread out across the sky. The best thing to do in that case is wait for the geometry to change. And it will, because GPS satellites are always on the move.

Good Geometry and Bad Geometry

You're no math whiz and GPS satellites aren't exactly visible to the naked eye. How do you know where the satellites are in the first place? How can you tell what's good geometry and what's bad geometry? That's why you have a GPS receiver.

You can check satellite geometry on the satellite status page—the one with the bar graph. Most GPS receivers display a "satellite plot" that looks like a shooting target with concentric rings around a bull's-eye. This is a bird's-eye view of your position, and you're at the center of the bull's-eye. Satellites located on the closest ring are directly overhead. Satellites located farther from the center of the bull's-eye are closer to the horizon.

The kind of geometry that gives the best accuracy is a nice, even distribution of satellites across the sky.

If the satellites are clustered in the same part of the sky, or if they're in a straight line, that's bad geometry.

DOP and EPE

Now that you understand the concepts, you won't have to think about it in the field when you're busy tracking game or trying to keep your balance on a narrow trail. To spot-check your position accuracy, all you have to do is glance at the satellite status or position page. Many GPS receivers display a number that evaluates the ever-changing satellite geometry called DOP (Dilution of Precision). The higher the DOP value, the less precise your positioning.

If your receiver doesn't give you a DOP value, it might display

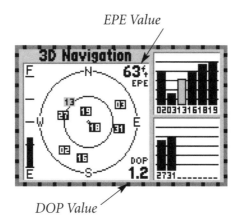

EPE Value

DOP Value

a generalized EPE (Estimated Position Error) reading instead. The EPE number tells you how far off the mark your receiver might be at any given moment, measured in meters or feet. It takes into account the DOP value (satellite geometry), as well as satellite signal quality and other sources of error already discussed. If your EPE is way off, then it might not be the best time to mark a waypoint.

In Summary

Since the first civilian GPS receivers hit the market more than a decade ago there's been confusion about their accuracy—and with good reason. So, in a nutshell, here are the undisputed facts:

• All GPS receivers are capable of getting you to within 15 meters (49 feet) of a known location, such as a waypoint, 95% of the time. Oftentimes they will give you much greater accuracy, sometimes less. It all depends on a variety of factors we've discussed in this chapter.

• WAAS-enabled GPS receivers are capable of 10- to 16-foot (3- to 5-m) accuracy.

• GPS receivers combined with a DGPS beacon receiver are capable of 3- to 10-foot (1- to 3-m) accuracy.

• Elevation or vertical readings are 50% less accurate than horizontal position error, up to 74 feet (22.5 m).

• More money does not buy more accuracy. All else being equal, such as number of channels, accuracy is not an issue between different brands and models of GPS receivers.

• The U.S. military no longer "scrambles" the GPS signal.

• More channels in your GPS receiver doesn't necessarily mean better accuracy.

CHAPTER 3

GPS Screen Pages

Like any shiny new gadget, your GPS receiver might seem a little intimidating at first. There's so much information on the screen! Don't worry, it's not as complicated as it looks. Now that you have a better understanding of how the technology works, it's a good time to get to know the main operating principles of the receiver itself. This chapter will help you navigate through the basic functions of any GPS receiver and determine what features are going to help you most in the field, and what features are just fluff. You'll know how to access key navigation information quickly, and how to customize your GPS receiver to suit your particular activities.

Paging through your GPS receiver can be an exercise in acronym overkill. There's XTE and CDI; BRG and SOG; ETE. And a dozen others. The thing to remember is that every number attached to an acronym has something to do with either speed, distance or time—or some combination of the three. Once you understand that, all those numbers your GPS receiver throws at you won't seem so confusing. A list of acronyms, definitions and their uses, is listed at the end of this chapter.

All that information on the screen might seem like overkill, but consider yourself lucky. In the old days, when GPS receivers were the size of toolboxes, their screens displayed a jumble of fluctuating numbers. Using one was like operating a computer from the 1970s, or an oversized calculator. There were no easy-to-understand graphics, no maps, no alarms. Just lines of text and numbers—nothing else.

Today's GPS receivers might be much more sophisticated in how they display those numbers, but the numbers have remained exactly the same. Every single piece of information crammed on the display of your GPS receiver has something to do with speed, distance, time or location. Once you understand that, it won't seem as confusing. And it'll be a lot easier to decipher all those crazy acronyms—like XTK, CDI, SOG, etc.—when you're navigating in the field. You'll get to know the handful of relevant readings and ignore the rest.

The truth is, all GPS receivers do the same thing. There's no difference in accuracy from one brand to the next. The same goes for basic operation. There are many more similarities between brands than there are differences. Why? Because all GPS receivers—whether they're WAAS-enabled, simply designed for pilots or optimized for boaters—compute only four kinds of measurements: speed, distance, time and location. And that information is located on a variety of "pages."

A "page" on your GPS receiver is another word for what's on the screen or display. Most GPS receivers have five main pages that organize and display the same information but in different ways. They are:

• *Satellite status page*

• *Position page*

• *Compass page*

• *Highway/Navigation page*

• *Map or Plotter page*

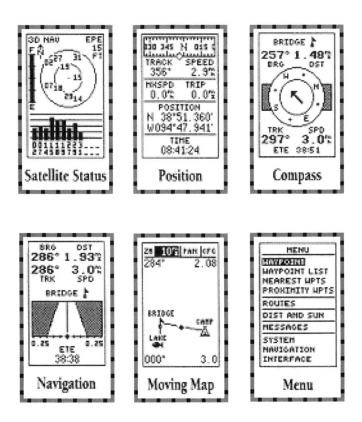

There are also *menu* and *submenu pages,* but you don't use them to navigate within the field. That is, they won't tell you where you're going and how to get there. But that doesn't mean menus and submenus aren't important. They're very important because they allow you to customize each page, access waypoints and routes, select the appropriate datum (information) when working with map or compass, and many other critical functions.

The pages used by all GPS receivers are linked in a continuous chain. If you started on the satellite status page and used the keypad to scroll through each page, you'd come back to the satellite status page.

The parts of a page that are divided into boxes are called "data fields." Data fields contain just about any kind of measurement your GPS receiver is capable of calculating.

Satellite Status Page

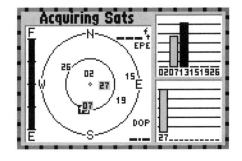

What's it good for?
Checking satellite signals; satellite geometry; battery life; EPE (Estimated Position Error).

When to use it?
Frequently, but for brief moments. Poor satellite reception and/or bad satellite geometry can occur at any time, during any activity, and this is where you go to check on it.

. . . .

Think of the satellite status page as the "behind the scenes" screen—you won't use it to navigate, but all the essential information about the health of the satellite constellation at any given moment can be found here. You're probably already somewhat familiar with the satellite status page. It's the one that pops up automatically when you turn on your GPS receiver.

Your receiver is constantly monitoring satellites. The display on the satellite status page depicts the activity in a bar graph. As new satellites come into view, a new bar appears in the graph. Bars that were solid five minutes ago may suddenly disappear as satellites pass out of view over the horizon. If a satellite is being monitored but not used to calculate a position, the bar appears hollow. On WAAS-enabled GPS receivers, the WAAS satellite signal strength is indicated by its own dedicated bar in the graph.

If you suspect your GPS receiver is having difficulty receiving signals, the satellite status page is the first place you want to go. For instance, if you're tracking game, you'll likely be moving through open fields into wooded areas and back into open fields again. Every time you pass from an open area with great satellite reception into an area capable of blocking satellite signals, it's a good idea to check the satellite status page. Make sure there are enough satellites in view to calculate an accurate position and keep a track log actively recording your trail. This is where you find EPE and DOP readings, which tell you at a glance how far off the mark you are.

Should I Stay or Should I Go?

To get an accurate reading of your present position, you don't have to be moving. In fact, the "position averaging" function, which increases the accuracy of a waypoint, requires that you remain motionless for at least a minute or two. However, to get accurate navigation measurements, such as current bearing, track or speed, you need to be moving.

Position Page

What's it good for? Confirming coordinates and datum; time and date; EPE.

When to use it? Infrequently, for brief periods. Mostly in planning with compass and maps; after marking a waypoint. No easy-to-understand graphics, like a compass rose, are displayed. Not ideal for field navigation.

• •

After you've acquired enough satellites to begin navigating, many GPS receivers automatically take you to the position page or the map page (if you have a built-in basemap). The position page is designed for easy identification of your present coordinates, altitude, map datum and EPE. Below the main field containing your immediate coordinates, the position page usually features a few boxes or "data fields" that display current speed, heading and perhaps a trip odometer. If you want, you can change the information shown in each box.

After marking a waypoint, you might be asked whether or not you want to activate the "position averaging" feature for a more accurate fix of your location. Many GPS receivers typically perform this function from the position page.

Because the position page highlights where you are at any given moment without any special graphics—no compass needle pointing the way, for example—it's best used while planning your next move in the field. For instance, you might want to find an easier route than you previously planned.

SPEED	TRIP TIMER
50.0ᵐ/ₕ	02:00
AVG SPEED	TRIP ODOM
20.0ᵐ/ₕ	40.0ᵐ/ᵢ
SUNRISE	SUNSET
07:07	05:54

N 41°31.970'
W081°38.348'

03:01:25
12-FEB-00

The first thing you need to do, then, is make sure your GPS receiver's coordinates match the datum specified on your topographic map, a task easily accomplished by consulting the position page.

Compass Navigation Page

What's it good for? Showing your direction of travel (track) as it relates to the direction of your destination (bearing); distance from destination; time to destination.

When to use it? Frequently, for extended periods. Navigating on land from point to point; navigating around obstacles; any time straight-line navigation isn't possible.

∙∙∙∙∙∙∙∙∙∙∙∙∙∙∙∙∙∙∙∙∙∙∙∙∙∙∙∙

Do not confuse the digital compass graphic on the compass page of your GPS receiver with a real compass. They may look the same, but they couldn't be more opposite in very important ways. Without movement—velocity or speed—your GPS receiver can't make sense of the world. It has no idea which way is north or south, up or down. It only knows where it is. This limitation is the strength of a compass. A compass can always tell you what direction you're facing, whether or not your feet are moving. That's because a compass has nothing to do with radio signals. Its needle is tuned to old-fashioned magnetic fields.

Electronic Compass

Because the compass page on your GPS receiver is not a real compass, it won't work when you stop moving. Some GPS receivers come with an electronic compass to give you an accurate heading when you're standing still. But these electronic compasses can't perform the functions of a true orienteering compass. Since they require batteries, they can't be relied on at all times.

But a compass can't tell you the latitude and longitude of where you're standing, not without a lot of work involving rulers, pencils, a good topographic map and some educated guesswork. This is the particular strength of a GPS receiver.

The compass page of your GPS receiver is full of information ideally suited to navigating on land. Why specifically on land? When's the last time you hiked a straight trail? Or drove more than a mile (km) or two without making a turn? Navigating on land means getting around obstacles. The obstacle can be as localized as a boulder or as big as a lake.

The advantage of the compass page is that it simultaneously shows your direction of travel (track) and the bearing (direction) to your destination. So when you're heading away from your destination due to some impassable obstacle, you will always know how to get back on course. The various data fields on the compass page display how long it's going to take to get to your destination, your current speed and so on.

Highway Navigation Page

What's it good for? Showing your direction of travel (track) as it relates to the direction of your destination (bearing); distance and time from destination; course deviation indicator (CDI).

When to use it? Infrequently for most land uses. Frequently for navigating on water from point to point; navigating over the road on an established route; any time straight-line navigation and higher speed is possible.

. . . .

Many GPS receivers give you the option of displaying either the compass page or the highway page, but they're both graphical representations of your position and where you're going. The main difference depends on how you want to get to your destination. The highway page is optimized for straight-line travel at higher speeds; the compass page, as we've seen, is best suited to stop-and-go travel where getting around obstacles is unavoidable. Using the highway page is as easy as keeping your car on the right side of the road.

The highway page is great for navigating open water, where straight-line travel is possible and even desirable. If your destination is a cove on the other side of the lake from the boat ramp, you don't want to waste time and fuel getting there. Assuming you already have the coordinates of the cove saved as a waypoint, you only need to press the "GoTo" key and hit the throttle. The graphic "highway" on the display will bend left or right to indicate which way you need to turn to keep a straight course.

Let's say you want to scout a few other favorite locations on the lake before you get to the cove. You can build a route linking several locations—an underwater rock pile, a dredging channel and so on—and go from point to point using the highway page. Each waypoint in the route appears as a signpost on the highway and the highway curves left or right to indicate the bearing between each waypoint.

Navigating a route using the highway page is like playing connect-the-dots. As with the compass page, the highway page also tells you how long it's going to take to get to each point, your current speed and so on.

1 ... 2 ... 3 ... Simulate!

You don't need to take your GPS receiver outside in order to practice with it. But it won't work inside your house, either. Not without giving you annoying warning messages every two minutes about having "Poor GPS Coverage." Every GPS receiver can "simulate" a position as if it were actually outside and receiving real satellite signals.

Just go to the setup menu and find the word "Simulate" or "Simulator" in the index. Scroll down, highlight it and press "Enter." Your GPS receiver is now in simulator mode, making it a lot easier to work with indoors. This is especially useful when planning a trip.

Map Page

What's it good for? Showing where you are in relation to other waypoints (a GPS receiver with no built-in map); where you are in relation to landmarks, such as roads, cities and bodies of water (receiver with a built-in map); where you are in relation to city streets, marine navaids, topo-graphic features (receiver with down-loadable maps).

When to use it? All the time.

· ·

The map page is sexy. It draws the eye. There's a good reason for that. We've been using maps for centuries. We know instinctively how to read them. And they're much easier on the eye than a jumble of numbers. The big advantage of an electronic map combined with a GPS receiver is that you can see, in real time, exactly where you are in relation to all the other features on the map. Before GPS came along, that wasn't possible.

Among the first people to recognize the huge implications of electronic mapping were captains of commercial vessels and airplane pilots. Both had radar, LORAN and other radio-navigation technologies to help them "see" what was around them. They could use this information to plot their location on a paper chart. But in a potentially dangerous situation there's no time to play around with protractors and pencils. Imagine an oil tanker navigating a narrow channel into a port hidden by a thick fog.

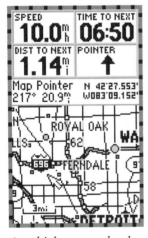

At a minimal zoom level, you don't see much detail on the map.

At a higher zoom level, you see more specifics on the map.

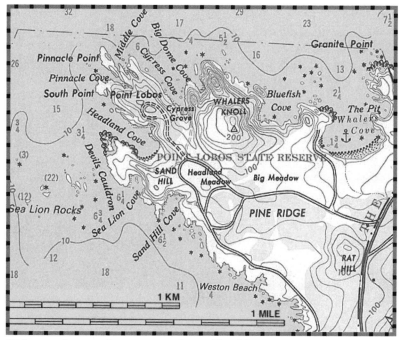

Unless you're a real expert, sea charts like this one can seem extremely complicated.

The captain stands in the wheelhouse, listening to the sonar ping off the sea floor. He's got one eye on the radar screen and another on the paper chart. The chart indicates large rock pinnacles rising from the sea floor. They could open the bottom of his tanker like a tin can. But where are they? Off his port bow? Starboard? Exactly how far ahead? Making matters worse, the tide is going out. He has less than 10 yards (10 m) of clearance. Forget it! He makes a wise decision and anchors outside the port until the weather clears and the tide rises again.

Today, our wise oil tanker captain would have a GPS chart-plotter in his wheelhouse, loaded with the newest NOAA (National Oceanic and Atmospheric Administration) sea charts. No doubt it would be connected to a DGPS beacon receiver to increase his position accuracy to within a yard (meter) or so. Despite the fog, he can see where he is at all times on the glowing map screen in relation to the rock pinnacles, the channel and the port facilities 2 nautical miles (3.7 km) away. He breathes a sigh of relief as his tanker slowly glides past the rock pinnacles hidden beneath the waves, keeping his keel over the deepest part of the channel.

You might not be hauling several million barrels of heavy crude through environmentally sensitive areas, but your map page is just as important to you as it is to the oil tanker captain.

Some GPS receivers have POI databases that give all kinds of information about specific waypoints.

At a glance, you can see where you are in relation to features on the map. Depending on what zoom level you're at—which is shown at the bottom of the page—these features might be roads or cities or entire continents. If your GPS receiver is capable of displaying more detailed downloadable maps, you might see elevation contours, or navigational aids such as lighthouses, even restaurants.

No matter what kind of map you're using, at lower zoom levels closer to the ground, you'll see a dotted line or "breadcrumb trail" tracing exactly where you've been.

Other than pinpointing where you are, you can create waypoints right from the map simply by moving the cursor over a feature and pressing "Enter" or "Mark." Building a route couldn't be easier.

Your map page also serves as a makeshift address book. By moving the cursor over certain POIs (Points of Interest) and hitting "Enter," crucial information pops up: phone numbers, addresses, navigation information that corresponds with a sea chart and so on.

Plotter Page

What's it good for? Showing where you are in relation to other waypoints.

When to use it? All the time.

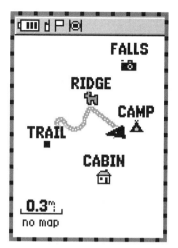

Plotter pages are great for showing where you are in relation to other waypoints.

If you don't have a built-in electronic map, you have a plotter page. GPS receivers that have a plotter page instead of a map page are ideal for someone who is already familiar with a particular area and needs only to mark waypoints for future reference, such as where camp is located, a secret fishing spot or a downed animal.

Basically, a plotter page is a map page without the map. Much like the map page, it shows waypoints, routes and track logs and where you are in relation to them. But it won't show roads, terrain features or anything that you haven't already saved as a waypoint.

The plotter page looks like the plotter on the satellite status page: a target ring of concentric circles set at regular intervals. At the center of the target is you, the triangle. The distance between each ring is noted in the corner of the page. As you zoom in close—100 feet (30 m), for example—your track log will be clearly evident and you will appear to be moving. At larger zoom levels—say, 25 miles (40 km)—however, you will appear almost stationary, especially if you're on foot.

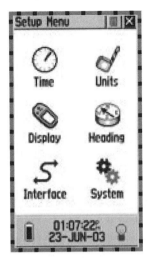

The main menu page is your first stop when customizing your GPS receiver's settings.

Submenus allow you to adjust things like map datums.

Menu Page

What's it good for? Customizing each page of your GPS receiver to give you the information you want; accessing waypoints and routes; finding POIs.

When to use it? All the time, but for brief periods.

. . . .

It might be considered the ugly sister of the other pages, but don't underestimate the importance of the menu page. This is the place to go when you need to tinker with the information displayed on your GPS receiver. Every single data field can be changed to give you the information you want.

For instance, if you're navigating through thick underbrush with the compass page displayed, you probably have no use for the XTE (Cross Track Error) reading. You can get rid of the XTE data field to show the bearing to your destination instead, much more useful. You do this by hitting the "Menu" key and finding the "Customize" or "Change Fields" option.

Let's say you're fishing on a bright day, so bright that it's hard to read the screen on your GPS receiver. Boosting the screen contrast first requires a trip to the menu page.

Want to find a particular waypoint or access a good route that you know has worked in the past? Go to the menu page.

The setup menu is yet another level of complexity accessible only through the menu page. This is where you customize your GPS receiver for your particular activity. If you're using a topographic map, you'll want to change your receiver's map datum to match the one used by the paper map.

The setup menu also allows you to swap miles for kilometers; adjust your receiver's output so you can download waypoints, track logs and routes to your computer; or, set your receiver to always reference true north instead of magnetic north.

Those are just a few examples. As you become more familiar with your GPS receiver, you'll find yourself scrolling through the menu page and setup menus like a pro.

Some typical terms and definitions.

JARGON	DEFINITION	WHAT IS IT REALLY?	RELEVANCE
BRG	Bearing	The compass heading to your destination— not the compass heading of current direction of travel.	Any land navigation when your course is constantly changing.
CDI	Course Deviation Indicator	Graphic representation of XTE (Cross Track Error), typically found on the highway page. Can be set to indicate small scale (meters) or large scale (miles) of deviation.	Best for sailing/boating and flying where keeping a set course from point to point is important.
CMG	Course Made Good	Compass direction from your starting point to your present position, or the ground you covered as you meandered toward your destination.	Probably won't use this too much.
COG	Course Over Ground	Same as CMG (Course Made Good).	Won't use this too much.

Continued on next page

JARGON	DEFINITION	WHAT IS IT REALLY?	RELEVANCE
CTS	Course to Steer	Compass direction you need to go to get where you're going that takes into account sea currents and headwinds—not a bearing, which is a straight-line indication to your destination.	Nautical/aviation term.
DOP	Dilution of Precision	A value of satellite geometry as it effects position accuracy. High DOP numbers mean less accuracy; low DOP numbers mean better accuracy.	All types and phases of navigation.
DST	Distance	How far you are from your destination, such as a waypoint or map feature.	All types and phases of point-to-point navigation.
DTK	Desired Track	Same as BRG (Bearing). The direction you want to be heading to get to your destination.	Hiking, hunting or any land navigation when your course is constantly changing.
EPE	Estimated Position Error	Position accuracy at any given moment based on satellite geometry, clock, ephemeris, multipath and atmospheric error.	All types and phases of navigation.
ETA	Estimated Time of Arrival	The time of day when you'll arrive at your destination, based on your current speed.	Straight-line navigation when your speed is relatively constant.
ETE	Estimated Time Enroute	How long it'll take to get from one point to another at a relatively constant speed and heading.	Won't use this too much.
HDG	Heading	Same as TRK (Track).	All phases of navigation for all activities.

JARGON	DEFINITION	WHAT IS IT REALLY?	RELEVANCE
SOG	Speed Over Ground	On land, same as speed. May differ from nautical speed due to sea conditions.	When straight-line travel is hampered by headwinds or waves.
SPD	Speed	How fast you're going at any given moment.	When straight-line travel is possible; driving, boating, sailing.
TRK	Track	The compass heading of your current direction of travel.	All types and phases of navigation for all activities.
TRN	Turn	Amount in degrees you need to turn to put you on a direct line of travel to your destination—not a bearing, which is a compass direction.	Nautical/aviation term.
TTG	Time To Go	How much time it'll take to get to your destination, based on current speed.	Won't use this too much.
VMG	Velocity Made Good	Speed at which you approach a destination, taking into account your present course. If you're not headed directly to your destination, VMG will be less than your present speed.	A speed reading better suited to hikers or any time direct point-to-point travel isn't possible.
XTE	Cross Track Error	How far off you are, left or right, from a direct line of travel between two points.	Best for sailing/boating and flying where keeping a set course from point to point is important.
XTK	Cross Track	Same as XTE (Cross Track Error)	Same as XTE

CHAPTER 4

Basic Navigation with GPS

This chapter addresses the basic navigation tools, terms and techniques that you will use in the field with GPS receiver, compass and paper maps. Hold on a second! Compass? Paper maps? The whole reason you bought a GPS receiver was to avoid compasses and paper maps! No problem. If you don't own a compass, you don't have to run out and buy one. Same thing goes for topographic maps.

Both of these technologies, however, are inexpensive and have been around for hundreds of years; long before GPS. And they'll be around for a few thousand more. Why? Because they've proven to be an effective means of navigation over and over and over again.

Digital Maps Versus Paper Maps

Digital maps have many advantages over paper maps (which we will discuss in depth in Chapter 6). But compared to the level of detail and resolution offered by 1:24,000- or 1:25,000-scale USGS topographic paper maps, the "basemaps" preloaded on any GPS receiver don't even come close. And you'll find the proprietary "topo" maps that you can buy and download into your GPS unit from a computer are often too general for true backcountry use.

Third-party software packages—from companies such as Maptech and National Geographic—are great for working with topographic maps on the computer; their resolution is fantastic. Unfortunately, you can't download them into your GPS receiver; only waypoints and routes can be downloaded from third-party digital maps.

So where does that leave you and your GPS receiver? With those old standbys, maps and compasses.

Tools of Backcountry Navigation

The main reason we're taking the time to discuss these "old" technologies is because GPS navigation techniques are based on navigation techniques developed for the map and compass and honed over time. The concepts of coordinate systems, map datums, taking your bearings and others began with map and compass. Why do you think your GPS receiver's software mimics the look of a compass even though it functions according to a completely different technology? The engineers who design GPS receivers aren't fools. They know that maps and compasses are familiar and intuitive to nearly everyone.

GPS has huge advantages over using a map and compass in the field, but GPS doesn't totally replace them. Any professional outdoorsman, angler, pilot or military person will tell you the same thing: Never rely on a single navigation technology alone. It's simply not safe. So what else do you need to know?

Topics we'll discuss include the following:

• *Observation*

• *Compass*

• *USGS topographic map*

• *Map tools*

Observation

Putting aside for a moment your GPS receiver, compass and map, how do you know where you are at any particular time? You use visual cues or landmarks. Your eyes are the best navigation tools you own—much better and more sophisticated than any gadget. For instance, you know that your home is 5 miles (8 km) south of the highway exit because you've driven that route a million times. You also know to turn left after the second light to get to your street. If you're coming from the opposite direction, say, from the grocery store instead of from work, then you should turn right at the light instead. Your little corner of the world is permanently etched on a cognitive map stored in your brain. You swear you could do it blindfolded—well, not quite.

You need real-world visual cues or landmarks to make sense of that cognitive map. Without visual landmarks you could get lost in your own living room. If you've ever stubbed your toe in the dark on a piece of furniture, you know what I'm talking about. That's essentially what happens when you go on a hike in unfamiliar backcountry. You're "blindfolded." And that's the whole point. That's why we love hiking in the backcountry, off the beaten path. Adventure is all about the thrill of discovery. Finding that idyllic trout pool, productive elk browse, or that one peak where you can get a fantastic view of the whole valley. Who wants to hike the same old trails all the time? Still, we don't want to be so nearsighted that we get lost. That's why having solid navigation skills is essential to enjoying the great outdoors.

While you may be metaphorically blindfolded in the backcountry, you're not blind. Navigating with a GPS, compass and map is all about recognizing and traveling between visual landmarks. The shortest route between two points, however, is almost never the one you're traveling on. This holds true for marine navigation as well. A straight line is a mathematical principle, not a backcountry reality.

Unfortunately it's also the principle by which your GPS receiver operates. Compass, too. If there's a sandbar or a canyon between Point A and Point B, your GPS receiver can't see it, even if the receiver has a digital map loaded into its memory. It will tell you that there are only 3 miles (4.8 km) separating you

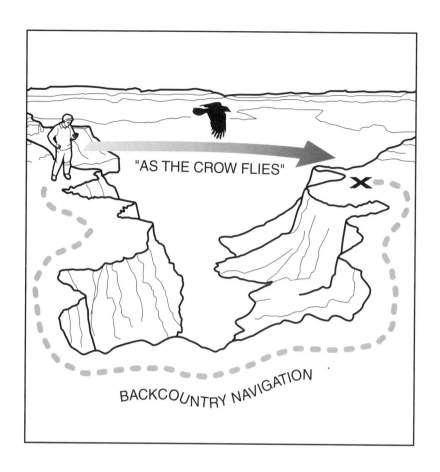

"AS THE CROW FLIES"

BACKCOUNTRY NAVIGATION

from your destination "as the crow flies," when in reality getting around that sandbar or canyon is going to take you 5 miles (8 km) off course.

Without a paper map for reference, a compass is at an even bigger disadvantage than a GPS receiver because it can't even tell you where you are in relation to your surroundings. In that case, you could wander 15 miles (24 km) off course and never know the difference.

Compass

So, observation can't do it all in the backcountry. You will benefit greatly from also using a compass.

For plotting locations on a map you need a good orienteering (or baseplate) compass with a rectangular, clear plastic base

Interference

GPS isn't the only technology susceptible to sources of interference that degrade accuracy. Compass needles are affected by the presence of metal objects and other magnetic sources. Try passing a pocket-knife or some metal object underneath the needle and watch it spin. When taking a bearing be sure to keep metal things like belt buckles, knives, cooking gear, vehicles, railroad tracks and power lines a safe distance away.

and rulers on its edges to help measure distances.

A direction-of-travel arrow extends vertically across the length of the baseplate.

The azimuth ring is a rotating plastic dial that shows cardinal headings—north, south, east, west—and all the headings in between, measured from 0 to 360 degrees.

Inside the azimuth ring is a liquid-filled vial that contains a floating magnetized needle. The red side of the magnetized needle always points toward magnetic north. This means you always know where all the other

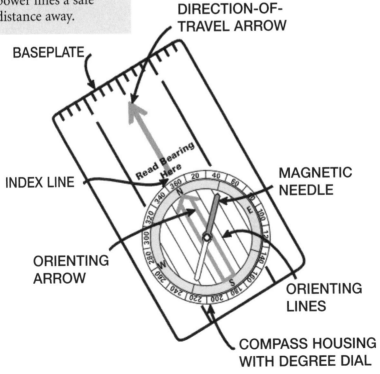

DIRECTION-OF-TRAVEL ARROW

BASEPLATE

INDEX LINE

Read Bearing Here

ORIENTING ARROW

MAGNETIC NEEDLE

ORIENTING LINES

COMPASS HOUSING WITH DEGREE DIAL

directions are in relation to magnetic north, making it a cinch to find the compass direction—or bearing—to any visible landmark.

The red arrow printed on the bottom of the vial is called the "north orienting arrow," or just "orienting arrow," which is used to align the azimuth ring when taking a bearing.

USGS Topographic Map

The most important element of successful navigation is planning your trip long before you lace up your hiking boots. And trip planning requires good maps and the skills necessary to read them.

Maps come in a mind-boggling variety of formats, from big road atlases that nearly everyone has used to highly localized trail maps you might find on the dusty rack of some outfitter's store in the middle of nowhere.

This is a detail from a USGS quad map.

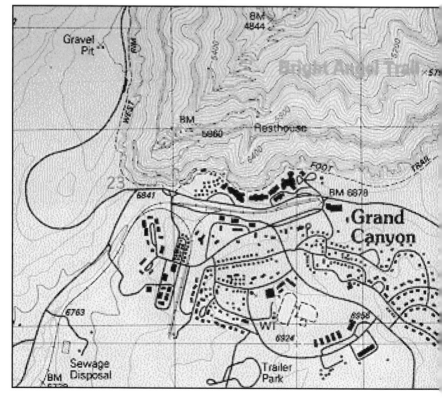

For our purposes the term "map" will always refer to a single type: the United States Geological Survey (USGS) 7.5-minute quadrangle topographic map, popularly known as a "quad map," or a "quad." USGS quad maps are the standard for back-country navigation.

Reading quad maps is an essential outdoors skill often taken for granted. Just because you can read a roadmap doesn't mean you can read a topographic map. It takes experience to use a topographic map correctly. But after some practice, you'll master it.

Digital mapping is the best thing to happen to GPS since powerful 12-parallel-channel receivers became the standard.

Almost every GPS receiver is marketed with at least a basic map embedded in its memory, and many GPS receivers have programmable flash memory that can store topographic maps downloaded from CD-ROMs. But remember that digital topographic maps distributed by GPS manufacturers for use with their receivers—so-called "proprietary" software—are not as detailed as standard USGS paper quad maps.

No matter how sophisticated GPS receivers become, they will always be limited by their display size and battery life. Paper maps have been around for thousands of years because they are a proven technology. You can't hand someone a GPS receiver and expect they'll know how to use it. You can't unfold an LCD display to get a broad sense of an area. And in all of human history, no paper map has ever shut down because its batteries ran out. You don't need a paper map if you have digital maps, of course, but both are at their best when used together.

Remember, a paper map can replace a digital map in the field, but a digital map cannot replace a paper map.

Where do you find a quad? To find the quad map you need, look for it on the Internet at www.usgs.gov, or look for it by name in one of the USGS state indices. USGS state indices are just big maps divided into smaller maps, but unlike most maps you're used to looking at, they don't have the usual landmarks—and there may be thousands of quads for any one state.

Where do you start? An easy trick is to find the location of your desired destination—say, a state park—on a standard road atlas. Due to the popularity of GPS receivers, most road

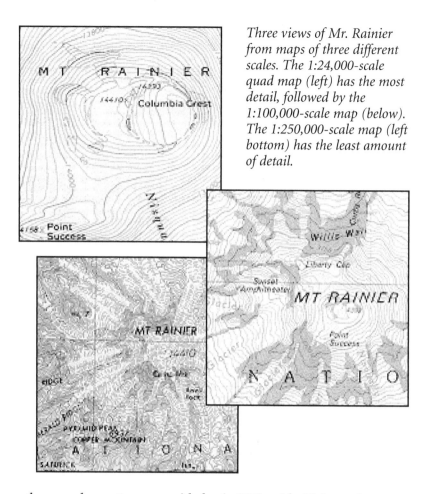

Three views of Mr. Rainier from maps of three different scales. The 1:24,000-scale quad map (left) has the most detail, followed by the 1:100,000-scale map (below). The 1:250,000-scale map (left bottom) has the least amount of detail.

atlases and gazetteers provide basic GPS grids. Using a few local reference points and this basic grid you can get the rough latitude and longitude of the state park. Then use these coordinates to find the exact quad you're looking for in the appropriate USGS state index.

What does a quad look like? It's printed on a single sheet of paper that represents a relatively small area, 6.5 by 8.5 miles (10.5 by 13.5 km) square. Each area is drawn to a "large" scale of 1:24,000 or 1:25,000. In map parlance, "large" scale maps such as quads contain the most detail of a limited area; "small" scale maps cover larger areas in more general detail. Think of it like this:

• *Large maps = small area, more detail*

• *Small maps = large area, less detail*

There's a quad map for almost every inch (cm) of the continental United States. Most of Alaska has been mapped at a scale of 1:63,360, with some populated areas also mapped at 1:24,000 and 1:25,000 scales.

A quad map provides detailed information about the locations of important landscape details such as buildings and most campgrounds, power lines, ski lifts, mines, footbridges, drawbridges, fence lines, private roads. These features are usually missing from maps in the smaller 1:100,000- to 1:250,000-scale ranges, which are typically limited to showing major features, such as boundaries, parks, airports, major roads, railroads, streams.

So what makes a quad map useful? It gives you a mental snapshot of your surroundings, the lay of the land so to speak. At a glance it's easy to see where the highest peak is in relation to the lowest valley or where impassable land features like wide rivers, swamps, canyons and lakes might stop you. A quad is ideally suited to planning a safe, efficient or even scenic route around, through or to any feature on the map, such as a peak or a waterfall.

A quad map isn't merely a detailed drawing, however. It's a tool that shows the distance and direction between any two places featured in its coverage area. In the field, figuring out your distance and direction to any point on the map requires the use of a compass and/or a GPS receiver. It takes a bit of practice, but the quad map makes this task a lot easier by providing a convenient graphic scale bar in the map margin that represents distances in miles, feet and kilometers.

More importantly, if you look closely at the edges of the map you'll see a series of numbers and tick marks used for determining the coordinates of any location on the map, including where you are at any given moment. Finding your location on a map is one of the most important backcountry navigation skills you can possess (you'll learn how to do it later in this chapter).

What's a map legend? This part of the map is the least appealing to the eye and yet the most important, and not just with the quad map. Why? Because a map legend tells you how to

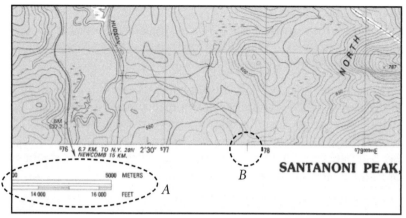

Quad maps provide a convenient graphic scale bar (A) in the map margin that represents distances in miles, feet and kilometers. Tick marks (B) indicate both the UTM and Lat/Lon grids are used for finding coordinates on the map.

read the map at hand. It'd be a bit like buying a French cookbook without a glossary of French cooking terms. Sure, you can try to make the dish according to the pictures, but it might not be edible.

The map legend (below) tells you when the map was made, what datum was used to make it, the map scale, contour interval, magnetic declination, among other things. Any time you use maps to plan a trip or find your location in

---

°30′
75°52′30″   690 000 FEET   WILLIAMSTOWN 5

Mapped, edited, and published by the Geological Survey

Control by USGS, USC&GS, and TVA

Topography from aerial photographs by photogrammetric methods
Aerial photographs taken 1958.   Field check 1960

Polyconic projection.   1927 North American datum
10,000-foot grid based on New York coordinate system, central zone
1000-meter Universal Transverse Mercator grid ticks,
zone 18, shown in blue

Fine red dashed lines indicate selected fence and field lines where
generally visible on aerial photographs.   This information is unchecked

Map photoinspected 1980
No major culture or drainage changes observed

the backcountry, you must first go to the legend in order to calibrate your compass and GPS so that everything works together. Otherwise you could end up plugging in coordinates that are way off the mark.

How accurate is a quad? We already know that GPS receivers aren't perfect when it comes to position accuracy. Nor are quad maps. That means positions plotted on a quad map with a GPS receiver, and vice versa, can be off by as much as 89 feet (27 m) horizontally (not including elevation) when the error possibilities of both are added together.

Don't be surprised if your GPS receiver (and its internal maps) and quad map don't put you smack on top of that mountain peak. Maps are subject to position error, too.

According to the USGS, 90% of all points tested on a quad map must be accurate to within $\frac{1}{50}$ inch (0.5 mm) on the map. At a scale of 1:24,000, that $\frac{1}{50}$ inch is equal to 40 feet (12 m).

The vertical accuracy standard requires that the elevation of 90% of all points tested must be correct within half of the contour interval. On a map with a contour interval of 10 feet (3 m), the map must correctly show 90% of all points tested within 5 feet (1.5 m) of the actual elevation.

Map accuracy might be less in areas covered by dense woodland or obscured by fog or clouds that prevent aerial photographs from providing precise detail.

We know that all GPS receivers can be off by as much as 49 feet (15 m) horizontally due to various unavoidable factors. Add map errors to the equation—39 feet (12 m)—and you end up with an error "budget" of 89 feet (27 m). The total error budget is somewhat larger for vertical accuracy. Errors in vertical or elevation readings displayed by GPS receivers are generally 50% greater than horizontal position error.

So, if your GPS receiver's horizontal error is 49 feet, its vertical accuracy is within 74 feet (22.5 meters). To the equation, add the quad map's vertical error, which is adjusted for a contour interval of 5 feet, although contour intervals differ with each map, and you end up with a total error budget of 79 feet (24 m). That 79 feet is how far you may be from your intended destination.

Map Tools

While not absolutely necessary for trip planning at home with a GPS receiver, compass and map, it's awfully handy to have a 3-foot (1-m) metal ruler (or at least an L-square ruler), some sharp pencils (with erasers), a waterproof pen and a transparent grid-overlay tool calibrated to measure UTM coordinates on a USGS map. It looks like a square ruler but is specially designed for working with topographic maps. They're inexpensive and available in most outdoors stores and they make it a lot easier to calculate precise position coordinates and distances on a quad map.

In the field all you need is a sharp pencil to mark up your map. Leave the steel ruler and pens at home. Packing the grid overlay tool (shown below, not to scale) is optional, but it takes up so little space you'll be glad you took it with you the first time you try to plot new map coordinates in the field.

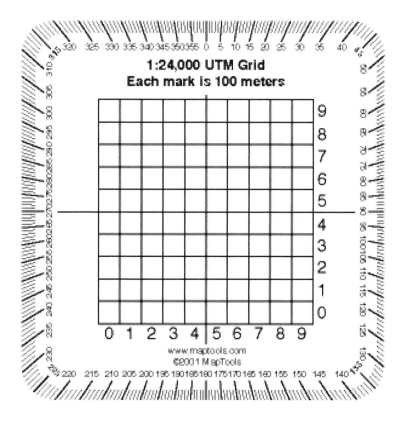

Terms of Backcountry Navigation

There are hundreds of navigation terms you'll pick up as you get more experience under your belt. But there are only three main concepts you need to understand in order to navigate with confidence in the backcountry. They are:

• *Map datums*

• *Coordinate systems*

Map Datums

A datum is a model or projection of the earth used by map-makers to create maps. It's sort of like a mathematical formula that matches the location of physical land features to abstract coordinates on a map. Sometimes it describes a small area and sometimes a datum describes the surface of the entire planet.

There are as many different kinds of datums as there are different kinds of people in the world, and people have been making maps for thousands of years. When you travel from one country to another, the datum one country might use to portray its particular corner of the world may be different than the datum used to draw maps in your own country. In fact, countries often issue maps that have been created using different datums to describe their own land area, including the United States. If this sounds confusing, that's because it *is* confusing.

The good thing is that the Global Positioning System can use an internationally recognized standard datum called WGS-84 (World Geodetic Survey 1984), and your GPS receiver automatically defaults to this datum. It's possible to go through your life never changing the datum in your GPS receiver.

Why should you care about datums? And when should you fiddle with them? If the datum in your GPS receiver doesn't match the map's datum, your coordinates will look the same but they'll be describing two totally different places on the map. Check the datum in your GPS receiver any time you plot a coordinate using a map, whether it's a quad map or a sea chart; or when you manually plug in coordinates from some other source. Change your datum to match the map's datum, which is listed in the map legend.

Changing the datum in your GPS receiver is as simple as changing your display to show meters instead of miles. Go to the setup menu and look under "navigation" or "system" or "units." Highlight the map datums box and scroll through the long list of datums to find the match to your map's datum.

Most USGS quads use one of two datums, the most popular being NAD-27 (some GPS receivers subdivide NAD-27 into several regional datums, but for navigating in the continental U.S., just choose NAD-27 CONUS). Quads that contain information from more recent surveys use the NAD-83 datum, which for all practical purposes is the same as WGS-84. At some point NAD-27 will be phased out altogether in favor of NAD-83, but not in our lifetime.

So how do you know what datum a particular USGS topographic map uses? That's easy. A good map—and all quad maps—always list the datum in the legend at the bottom of the sheet.

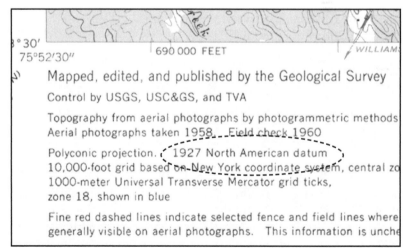

USGS topographic maps list the datum in the legend at the bottom of the sheet (circled).

Datum did 'em in: A cautionary tale

Let's say you're hunting caribou in Alaska. You're headed down a trail when Pete, your hunting buddy, comes running from the opposite direction. "There's a giant grizzly and two cubs eating a dead caribou 2 miles [3 km] down the path," he blusters. "Better turn around!"

Pete tends to exaggerate things, but still, what's the harm in swapping waypoints with him, just in case? At least Pete was smart enough to mark the position of the grizzly, which he reads off to you before he runs back to camp. You plug the coordinates into your GPS receiver, set a proximity alarm that will warn you when you're within 500 yards (450 m) of the new waypoint, and down the trail you go, confident that you won't be surprised by an ugly encounter with a grizzly—if there ever was a grizzly in the first place.

Twenty minutes later, as the grizzly is dragging your body through the brush, you curse Pete for giving you the wrong coordinates. But it's not Pete's fault. The datum in his GPS receiver was set for NAD-27 Alaska; whereas yours was set for WGS-84.

You didn't confirm datums with Pete's GPS receiver, and now look at you....

There may also be information on how much to shift a position to convert it to NAD-83. That number is the amount of error that will affect all your waypoints if you leave your GPS receiver set to its WGS-84 default. In the Continental United States the difference between WGS-84 and NAD-27 can be as much as 200 yards (180 m).

Coordinate Systems

We all know how to find ourselves on a globe, or our address on a street map, but how do you translate locations and addresses into the language of "positions" that your GPS receiver uses?

To define your location on any map you have to use a recognized coordinate system. Coordinate systems don't care about mountains and valleys and oceans and rivers the way that map datums do. Unlike most map datums, coordinate systems aren't regional either. They are mathematical formulas that treat the earth as if it were a featureless ball, dividing its surface into sections and subsections—a grid—until every square inch (cm) of the earth has its own unique address or "position" where lines of the grid intersect.

Whereas the earth is round, the grid is flat in order to simplify the use of maps and to avoid the inconvenience of pinpointing locations on curved surfaces. This rectangular grid consists of two sets of parallel lines perpendicular to each other.

Therefore, all coordinate systems have three main parts: a vertical axis, a horizontal axis and a unit of measurement. The two main coordinate systems are:

• *Latitude and Longitude (Lat/Lon)*

• *Universal Transverse Mercator (UTM)*

Lat/Lon Coordinate System. This is the standard system of measurement used on most maps throughout the world, and it is the primary system for marine and aviation navigation. This coordinate system uses the center of the earth as a reference point, from which a system of horizontal and vertical lines are laid on the earth's surface. The resulting grid is designed so that any point on the earth can be designated by its latitude and longitude.

The horizontal axis, or reference line, is the equator. The vertical axis or line of reference is called the Prime Meridian, which connects both the North and South Poles and passes through Greenwich, England. Positions between these imaginary lines are defined by using a series of horizontal lines, called parallels of latitude north or south of the equator; and meridians of longitude, which define the value of a position east or west of the Prime Meridian. The unit of measurement for Lat/Lon, as with any circle, is degrees.

Everybody's doing the GPS grid

As GPS becomes more and more popular, typical maps that everyone uses, such as road atlases and street maps, are being marketed with terms like "GPS grids included." Does that mean you can take a Lat/Long coordinate from a road map and plug it into your GPS receiver? Yes and no.

Road atlases and official-looking gazetteers aren't required to maintain the same high standards of accuracy that USGS maps do. Such simplified grid references are fine for general city-to-city navigation. My advice? Don't use these maps for precise backcountry positioning or street-level navigation.

"Lines of longitude are long." Completely arbitrary, I know but that's how I remember which way lines of longitude run. Think of a typical map configuration; the North Pole is depicted above the South Pole; and North America is above South America. Lines of longitude, or meridians, run north and south across the continents and just seem longer than lines of latitude. But that's just me. Use whatever works for you.

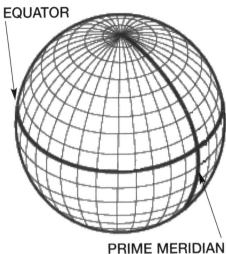

EQUATOR

PRIME MERIDIAN

Lines of longitude run between the North and South Poles and are used for measuring points east or west of each meridian. The Prime Meridian is assigned the value of 0 degrees, and meridians to the west of the Prime Meridian are measured in degrees west; likewise those to the east of the Prime Meridian are measured by their number of degrees east.

"Lines of latitude are fat." Not very precise, but that's how I remember which way lines of latitude run, like a belt around the waist of a fat man. Lines of latitude, or parallels, run perpendicular to lines of longitude beginning at the equator—think of the equator as a big belt, which wraps around the entire earth. It's also assigned a value of 0 degrees. Lines of latitude measure points north or south of the equator right up to each pole.

At the equator, one degree of latitude and one degree of longitude equals about 69 square miles (180 sq km). Together they make a big square if we only measured positions in whole degrees. That's sort of like using hours instead of seconds to determine the winner of a hundred-yard dash. So, to get more precise measurements, degrees of latitude and longitude are divided further into minutes and seconds. Each degree has 60 minutes, and each minute of each degree has 60 seconds. By using degrees, minutes and seconds as a measurement, a position can be defined accurately anywhere on the planet.

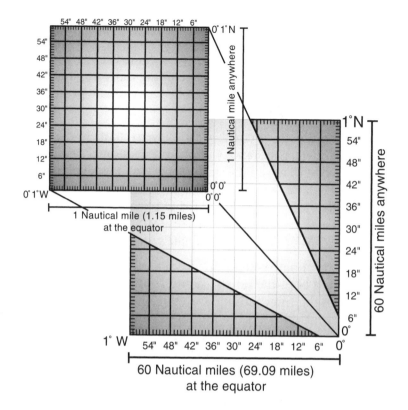

Here's a typical Lat/Lon pair of coordinates:

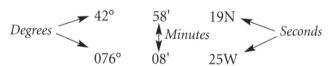

These coordinates just so happen to be in central New York State, and are expressed in degrees/minutes/seconds. You can also display Lat/Lon coordinates in a format called decimal degrees for more precise measurements. In your setup menu, just select "Lat/Lon" as your coordinate system, then choose "ddd.mm.mmm" for decimal degrees. Below is an example of Lat/Lon coordinates expressed in decimal degrees. Although the coordinates appear different than those above, they are in fact the same position.

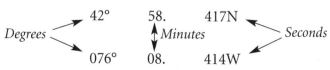

UTM Coordinate System. After Lat/Lon, the second most popular coordinate system is the Universal Transverse Mercator (UTM) system. Like GPS technology itself, the UTM grid was developed by the military and it's becoming more popular with hunters and hikers. Why? Finding your approximate position on a map at a glance is far quicker and easier than using Lat/Lon.

The UTM coordinate system also lets you zero-in on an exact map location and calculate distance without any additional steps or conversions. Best of all, it's the simplest system to use with your GPS receiver and topographic quad map, which we'll demonstrate later in the chapter when we use UTM to plot a location. (If you're not working with maps it doesn't make any difference whether you use the UTM or Lat/Lon coordinate system.)

The UTM coordinate system divides the earth into sixty equal zones covering both the northern and southern hemispheres, starting from the International Dateline and progressing eastward. Each zone is assigned a number from 1 to 60. For instance, the continental U.S. is covered by ten zones, from Zone 10 on the West Coast through Zone 19 on the East Coast. Each zone is a strip measuring six degrees of longitude in width.

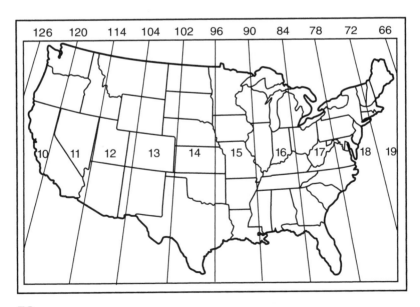

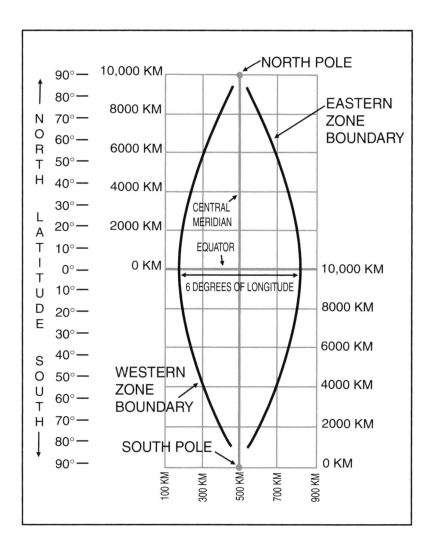

A "central" zone meridian runs through the middle of each zone and is assigned a value of 500,000 meters. This is the vertical axis (like the Prime Meridian is for the Lat/Lon coordinate system). The horizontal axis of each zone is the equator.

Positions within the northern hemisphere of a UTM zone are always defined by their distance east or west from the zone meridian, or the "easting" of the position. This is followed by the position's distance north from the equator, or "northing" of the position.

Easting and northing are not the simplest terms to understand, I know, but it's like the Metric system. Once you get the hang of it, it makes a lot more sense. Just remember these facts:

• Easting is a position's distance east or west from the zone meridian.

• Northing is a position's distance from the equator, which is measured from 0 in the northern hemisphere.

• A zone meridian has a value of 500,000 meters, therefore:

• Coordinates with easting values less than 500,000 are always west (to the left) of the zone meridian, and

• Coordinates with easting values more than 500,000 are always east (to the right) of the zone meridian.

Compared to traditional Lat/Lon coordinates, UTM coordinates such as those shown below might seem awkward and strange, and probably a little bit intimidating. That's a natural reaction; so let's take the mystery out of it. A set of UTM coordinates is made up of three basic parts: the zone number and hemisphere; the easting value; and the northing value.

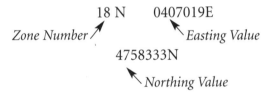

Once you consider that all UTM values are measured in meters, it all starts to come together. The position of the coordinates listed above can be found in Zone 18.

Okay, that's a start, but this is still quite a large strip of the planet. At a glance we can greatly narrow the possible area where these coordinates might be located because the easting value of 407,019 is less than 500,000. Therefore it must be west of Zone 18's meridian. And the "N" next to the zone number tells us that we're in the northern hemisphere.

Can we get closer? Sure, measure 92,981 meters (500,000 − 407,019 = 92,981) west of Zone 18's meridian for the easting baseline. That puts us on the East Coast somewhere.

Finding exactly where the northing baseline falls is even easier. Just go 4,758,333 meters north from the equator. And that puts us in the northern U.S.

Where the northing and easting baselines intersect is the precise location of these coordinates. And they turn out to describe the very same location in central New York State that we used for our Lat/Lon coordinates earlier in the chapter.

Lat/Lon or UTM? The easy answer is whatever you're comfortable with. USGS quad maps come with both Lat/Lon and UTM grid marks. If you're not working with maps, then it really doesn't matter which coordinate system you use.

The factory default for most GPS receivers is Lat/Lon and you could get along fine without ever changing it. For aviation and marine use, Lat/Lon is the standard because planes and ships cover large distances in a single journey and don't often have a need for navigating short routes in relatively small areas. But I prefer using UTM because it's easier to understand and easier to use on the fly.

Conversion Aversion

Backcountry navigation occurs in a tiny slice of the world with large-scale maps that have lots of detail. Finding your location at a glance on such a crowded map is a nice benefit of the UTM coordinate system. Since coordinate values are tied directly to a distance measurement (meters), as opposed to time (degrees/minutes/seconds), you can tell how far apart two positions are in the same zone without even looking at a map. And there's no messy conversion of degrees, seconds and minutes into a distance measurement as is necessary with the Lat/Lon coordinate system.

Converting UTM coordinates to Lat/Lon coordinates, and vice versa, involves a lot of math. Your GPS receiver can serve as a handy conversion calculator. Simply plug in the coordinates as a waypoint using either UTM or Lat/Lon, then change the coordinate system in the setup menu. Look up the waypoint from memory and it will be displayed in the new coordinate system.

Techniques of Backcountry Navigation

Navigating the backcountry with a GPS receiver, compass and maps can involve a wide range of techniques and tricks that apply to a staggering variety of potential situations (getting lost, sudden whiteouts, hunting with a group and so on) and activities (mountain climbing, snowmobiling, birdwatching, etc.). Here are a few important basics that form the core of navigating in all environments, no matter what you're doing in the backcountry:

- *Preparing topographic maps*
- *Adjusting the compass for magnetic declination*
- *Taking a bearing*
- *Plotting your location*
- *Recording bearings on a map*
- *Entering coordinates from a map into your GPS receiver*
- *Taking coordinates from a GPS receiver and applying them to a map*

Map Preparation

The map we'll use is a USGS quad titled "Redfield, N.Y." Before we start marking it up, let's take a look at the margins of the map (below). All those numbers and tick marks indicate either measurements in degrees of Lat/Lon or UTM values. The implied grid between these tick marks isn't actually printed on the map, so we're going to draw one ourselves. Why? Because making the grid visible on the map features

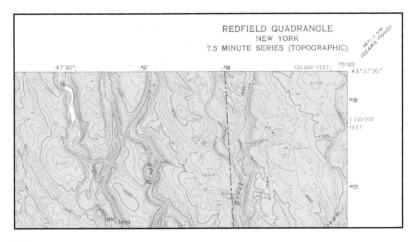

will make it much easier to locate and precisely measure coordinates.

We're only going to draw a UTM grid and make all our measurements in UTM. This is because of the many advantages that the UTM coordinate system offers over Lat/Lon. And because we can easily convert Lat/Lon coordinates into UTM coordinates with our GPS receiver if we need to.

You'll notice light blue tick marks at regular 1,000-meter (1,090-yard) intervals in the margins of the map. Next to them are the corresponding northing or easting values (Lat/Lon tick marks are always black). If there isn't a UTM value labeled next to a tick mark, check for it on the opposite side of the map. These intermediate UTM values are abbreviations for the complete UTM value: The last three zeroes have been dropped. Later, you'll determine those last three digits of a complete set of UTM coordinates using a grid overlay tool.

Tick marks used for measuring distance always extend from the edge of the map outward into the blank margin—ignore dashes that extend from the map edge into the map.

The entire area represented by the map is indicated by the complete northing and easting marks printed on the bottom right (below) and top left corners of the map sheet. You'll need to consult these complete UTM values when the time comes to take coordinates from the map and enter them into your GPS receiver; or when you want to take coordinates from your GPS receiver and plot them on the map.

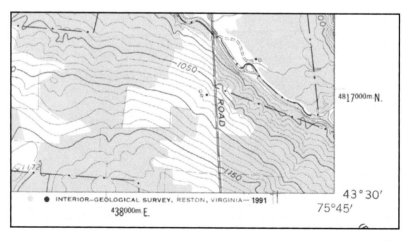

The first time you draw a UTM grid on a quad map you'll wonder where your tax dollars are going. Can't the USGS afford enough light blue ink to do it themselves?! Well, no, but they're slowly making progress. Until they finish the job, it's up to us. So, find a nice flat surface and roll out the map. Lightly tape down the corners so the map won't move.

Get your steel ruler and start from the bottom with the northing tick marks. Why there? Because northing baselines are shorter and the task won't seem so tedious by the time you get to drawing the easting baselines, which are longer.

I prefer to draw baselines with a hard-leaded colored pencil (red) of the sort used by sketch artists. You can use a pen, but make sure the point is fine enough not to obscure fine map details, because Murphy's Law dictates that the coordinates you want will always be underneath the ink. Also, choose a pen with waterproof ink or your nice, neat grid will smudge from rain, dew or moist body heat, further obscuring details of the map. A mechanical pencil works well, but I find that pencil lead is a little difficult to see in certain light.

Now, start lining up those tick marks and draw! Keep in mind that UTM grid lines won't be exactly parallel with the edges of the map. When you're done, roll up the map and put it aside. Coffee mugs have a way of appearing out of thin air on top of maps left out in the open.

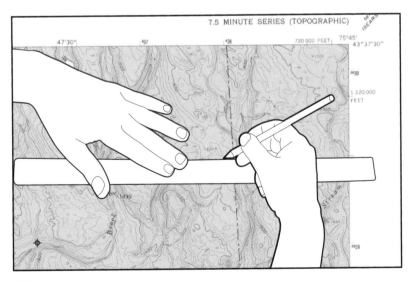

Adjusting for Magnetic Declination

This section only applies to compasses, and only in the instance when a compass is being used in conjunction with a topographic map. When you use a compass and map together it's critically important to adjust your compass to the map's idea of "north." You see, your compass needle always points toward magnetic north, which is located on Canada's Bathurst Island in the Arctic Ocean. However, topographic maps are based on true north. All the lines on it, from bottom to top, converge on the geographic North Pole.

The difference between your map's north and the north your compass needle points toward is called "magnetic declination." You have to account for this difference by

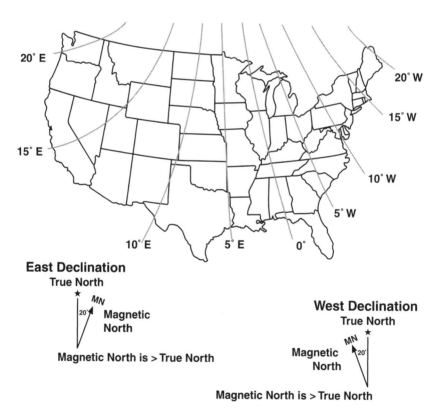

Magnetic variation isn't consistent across the country, and your compass needs to be adjusted for it or your bearings will be off by as much as 20 degrees.

adjusting your compass according to the declination scale located at the bottom of the map sheet. Otherwise, any coordinates or bearings you plot on the map will be signigicantly off the mark.

Although it's possible, there's no reason to change the north reference in your GPS receiver, which defaults to true north.

The magnetic force that makes your compass needle spin varies from place to place, state to state, country to country. This variance isn't entirely predictable, but the good people at the USGS print declination scales on all their topographic maps to help you adjust your compass. The scale at the bottom of our Redfield quad map indicates that the difference between true north and magnetic north is 12 degrees west (below).

Adjusting a compass so it works with a map is very easy, but first check your owner's manual. Most compasses allow some way to rotate the red orienting arrow—not the magnetic needle—until it points to the correct offset shown on the declination scale. Once the orienting arrow is adjusted, all the coordinates and bearings you take from the map, and any bearings you take in the field and apply to the map, will be automatically oriented to true north. No adding or subtracting.

If your compass doesn't allow you to turn the orienting arrow, or if it doesn't even have an orienting arrow, you will have to

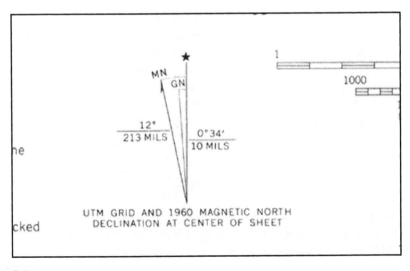

UTM GRID AND 1960 MAGNETIC NORTH
DECLINATION AT CENTER OF SHEET

add or subtract degrees when plotting bearings on the map. In our example, we will add 12 degrees. That's the rule for west declinations. If the declination was 12 degrees east instead of west, you would have to subtract 12 degrees. The old standby rhyme for remembering this formula is: "West is best, east is least." Add degrees for west declinations; subtract degrees for east declination.

Taking a Bearing

Now that your compass is adjusted, you can take a bearing in the field. A bearing is simply the direction to a landmark expressed in degrees. Taking a bearing is the foundation for 99% of all wilderness navigation. A bearing indicates a direction of travel, and when plotted on a map, it can be used to get a position fix.

It's very simple to take a bearing. Let's say we wanted to know the direction—or bearing—from our present position to the top of a distant peak.

Here are the steps to get the job done:

• Face the peak.

• Hold the compass level, centered a little above your waist, with the direction-of-travel arrow pointing away from your body and toward the peak.

• Try to zero-in on a specific area of the peak. For instance, if it has one sloping face and one steep face, point the direction-of-travel arrow at one or the other.

• Rotate the azimuth ring until the red orienting arrow lines up with the red end of the floating magnetic needle.

• Read the number on the azimuth ring at the spot where it touches the direction-of-travel arrow. This is your bearing expressed in compass degrees. That's the direction you need to travel to get to the peak.

Remember, you can't take a bearing with a GPS receiver, at least not in the traditional sense. Every single bit of information your GPS receiver displays, including the direction you're traveling, is based on movement or velocity. If you stand still with a GPS receiver it can't tell you which way is north, south, east or west.

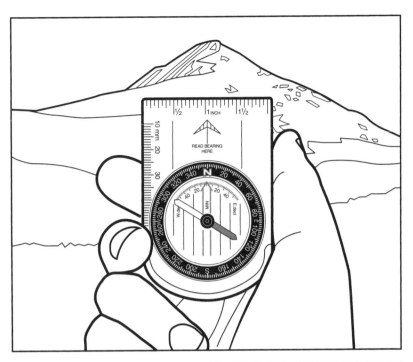

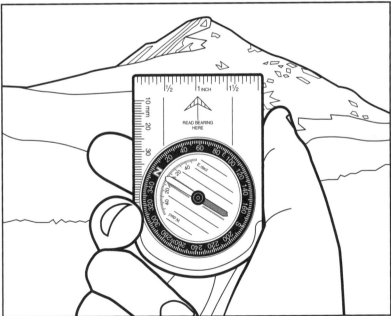

In the top illustration, the two arrows are not aligned. In the bottom illustration, the azimuth ring has been adjusted so both the orienting arrow and the magnetic arrow are aligned.

It can only tell you where you are. It can, however, give you a bearing between your present location and a waypoint stored in its memory if you hit the "GoTo" function to that waypoint.

But landmarks that are not saved as waypoints—say, a mountain peak in the distance—are invisible to your GPS receiver. It has no idea what bearing to take to get to that peak.

If you start walking toward the peak, the compass rose on your navigation page rotates so that you can take a bearing. But it's not exactly convenient to simultaneously walk, sight a landmark and watch the screen on your GPS receiver in order to get a bearing. That's a recipe for a sprained ankle.

Since a compass works on magnetism it doesn't require you to be moving to indicate a direction to a landmark. But a compass can only tell you which direction is north, south, east or west. It doesn't know your position. You can take multiple bearings with a compass, then apply these bearings to a map and triangulate your position, but that's a tedious process that only results in an approximate position. And you need ideal conditions to sight enough landmarks, to say nothing about featureless landscapes such as deserts and large bodies of water. A GPS receiver, on the other hand, shows your exact position at any given moment, in any weather, day or night.

Plotting Your Location

The technique used to plot your location on a map with a compass is the same technique your GPS receiver uses to determine its location: by triangulating from known reference points. Your GPS receiver, of course, uses satellite signals. With map and compass you have to sight at least two—three is best—recognizable landmarks that also appear on your map. This isn't always easy. The terrain might not offer enough suitable landmarks; the geometry of the landmarks, where they are in relation to you, might be poor; it could be pouring rain, foggy, or wind might blow your map around. You can forget about doing it at night. Or, maybe you're just not very good at matching what's on a map to your surroundings.

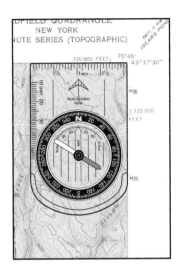

Recording Bearings on a Map

The first thing you need to do in the field is orient your map so that its perspective matches the physical features of the landscape (north on the map is actually facing north in the field). To do that, place the edge of your compass at the corner of the map's edge with north or 0 degrees intersecting the direction-of-travel arrow. Rotate the map and compass together until the red end of the compass needle aligns with the red end of the orienting arrow. Now you can more easily compare map features with physical landscape features.

Next, look around for good landmarks (below). Unique things, such as microwave towers, bodies of water, buildings, water tanks, roads, mountain peaks, make good points of reference. Select at least three as far apart from each other as possible, not clustered together, and take a bearing from each one.

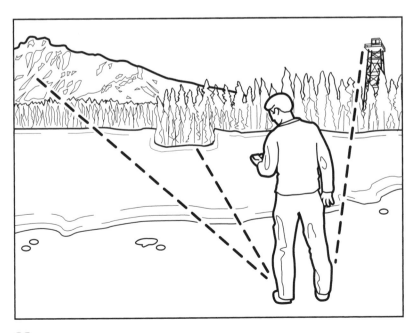

Let's start with the mountain peak in the illustration.

The third step depends on the kind of compass you have, but the idea is basically the same. Place the compass edge lengthwise so the long edge touches the peak as it appears on the map, with the travel arrow pointing toward it, not toward you. Now pivot the compass, keeping the edge on the peak, until the magnetic needle lines up with the orienting arrow.

Use the edge of the compass touching the peak and draw a line on the map from the peak toward you. You are somewhere on this baseline. Not very precise, but we're getting there.

To narrow the possibilities, take a cross bearing from another landmark, perhaps the microwave tower in the distance. Draw a new baseline on the map using the same process.

Theoretically, you are located where these two baselines intersect. But taking visual bearings isn't an exact science and you're guaranteed to have errors. So, repeat the process a third time if possible. The end result should be a small triangle bordered by your three baselines. Your location is somewhere inside that triangle. The smaller the triangle the better job you did in sighting your bearings and plotting them on the map (below). If the triangle is unusually large, try again.

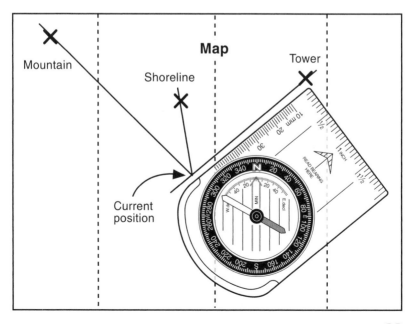

Entering Coordinates from Map to GPS

The best way to do this is with digital mapping software. Just point, click and download! Ah, but we can't drag our computers with us into the backcountry.

Let's say I'm on a hike when I notice that a mayfly hatch is on. There's no way I could've predicted a mayfly hatch while I was planning my hike from the computer. I realize that I'm hiking somewhere near this great little brook that's probably going crazy with rainbow trout hitting the mayflies. The brook's location isn't loaded as a waypoint in my GPS receiver, but that doesn't mean I can't get the coordinates from my quad map right here in the field. Then I can enter them into my GPS receiver and go straight to the stream the next time I'm in the area.

When I hiked this area last year I noticed a short section of Cold Brook that had nice, deep trout pools in it. The location is indicated by the crosshairs that I marked on the map detail below, which is taken from the USGS "Redfield" quad that I had prepared earlier by drawing guidelines on it. But let's look at the map without the UTM grid, just to see how close we can get to the actual coordinates by eyeballing the tick marks.

Don't forget that the UTM values that correspond with the tick marks on the map are shown in abbreviated form—the last three zeros have been dropped. Also, the different sizes of the numbers don't mean anything. They're printed that way to make them easier to read.

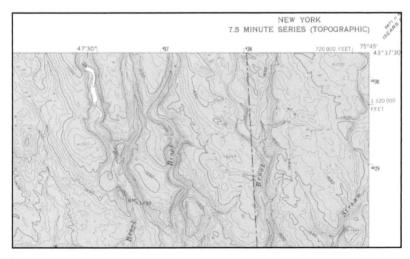

Okay, our trout pool looks to be about three-quarters of the way east of the 435-easting tick, and almost on top of the 4828-northing tick, maybe a bit above it. We know from drawing our UTM grid that these two ticks intersect to form a 1,000-meter square. In that case, three-quarters of 1,000 is 750 meters, which we'll use to complete our easting value. And if we add about 100 meters to the complete northing value of 4828, that should put us a hair above the tick where we first eyeballed it.

So the complete, eyeballed set of UTM coordinates of the trout pool are (the underlined numbers are the eyeballed part of the coordinates; they don't appear underlined in the GPS receiver):

18 N 0435750E
　　　 4828100N

Using our eyeballed coordinates to navigate by, I could easily walk along the creek bank until I hit the fork where the little feeder stream comes into Cold Brook from the north. But that little stream could be dried up this time of year and I could just as easily walk right by the trout pool. I want to make sure I get there while the mayfly hatch is still on, so I'm going to use my grid tool for an exact measurement.

All I have to do now is lay my UTM grid tool over the square formed by the baselines that I drew on the map earlier. For the northing value, count the number of meters up or north from baseline 4828: 51 meters. And for the easting value, count the

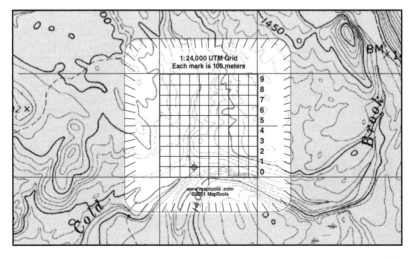

number of meters to the right or east of baseline 435: 745. Add everything together, and the complete, precise set of UTM coordinates of the trout pool are (the underlined numbers are the part of the coordinates we measured using the grid tool; they don't appear underlined in the GPS receiver):

18 N 0435745E
4828051N

Did you notice how close we got to the exact location of the pool just by eyeballing the coordinates using the UTM tick marks and some simple math? We were merely 5 meters (16 ft) too far east (750 – 745 = 5), and 49 meters (53 yds) too far north (100 – 51 = 49). Not bad! There's no way I could've guessed a position that close by eyeballing Lat/Lon coordinates!

After double-checking that the datum in my GPS receiver matches the map's datum (NAD-27), and confirming the correct UTM zone in the map legend (18), it's merely a matter of entering the precise UTM coordinates as a new waypoint into my GPS receiver and I can start navigating to the trout pool.

Entering UTM coordinates into your GPS receiver might be confusing the first time you try it. That's because they're often displayed differently between competing brands of GPS receivers. Maps also display UTM values differently (in abbreviated form) than how your GPS receiver might display them. Just remember these four rules and your UTM coordinates will always point to the right place:

• Don't forget to enter the correct UTM zone first, which is listed in the map legend.

• Ignore the number sizes. They're only used to make UTM coordinates easier to read, with no bearing on their values.

• If your GPS receiver allows seven digit places for the easting value, but your easting value is only six digits long, the first digit is always zero. To ease confusion, some GPS receivers allow only six digits for the easting value, in which case the additional zero is implied.

• Some receivers require that you input a letter after confirming the zone number. Enter either "N" if you're north of the equator or "S" if you're south of the equator. Do not enter any other letter or your GPS receiver might save your coordinates in the wrong hemisphere. You'll be trout fishing in Argentina instead!

Plotting Coordinates from GPS to Map

Once while hiking east of Mad River, I saw this great little section of Cold Brook that had nice trout pools. Does this sound familiar? Well, this time I was smart enough to save the location as a waypoint. But I didn't label the waypoint, instead allowing the GPS receiver to assign a default name. I think the trout pool might be the waypoint labeled "WPT019," but I can't be sure.

The problem is that my GPS receiver has dozens of mysterious waypoints in its database with similar names. What can I say? I'm lazy and I don't always label my waypoints. The only way to be certain is to plot the coordinates from the GPS receiver onto the map.

18 N 0435745E
    4828051N

The process is exactly the same as the one we demonstrated when taking coordinates from the map, except in reverse. First, make sure that the datum in the GPS receiver matches the datum on the map (NAD-27), and that the zone numbers are the same (18).

If the waypoint was saved in Lat/Lon coordinates, just switch the coordinate system to "UTM" in the setup menu and recall the waypoint as a UTM position.

Locate the 435 easting and 4828 northing tick marks on the map. Eyeball the general location where they intersect. This is enough to jog my memory of the WPT019's location, but I want to be absolutely certain.

I know that I should put one corner of the UTM grid overlay tool to the right or east of the baseline that I drew on the map earlier because the easting value is greater than 43500. I also know I should put the other edge of the tool above or north of the 4828 baseline because the northing value is greater than 4828000.

All that's left to do is count 745 meters east and 51 meters north and scratch an X on the map where the two lines intersect. Ah yes, that must be the place, right at the fork where the little feeder stream flows into Cold Brook from the north.

Now might be a good time to mend my lazy ways and rename WPT019 to something more meaningful, like "Trout."

CHAPTER 5

Hunting or Hiking with GPS

Two popular outdoor activities that have benefited most from GPS technology are hunting and hiking. On the surface they might not seem to have a lot in common. Hunters go to the same spot in the woods at the same time every year and wait around for animals, right? And what do hikers do besides walk around aimlessly from Point A to Point B? Both hunting and hiking are a bit more complicated, of course, and the closer you look you begin to realize these pursuits have a lot more in common than you might initially think.

Hunting occurs in particular seasons. The sport of hunting, however, is a year-round process that involves regular trips to the backcountry to track the movements of game animals. Hiking might not be as goal oriented as hunting, but coordinating a 50-mile (80-km) hike with a group of friends split up over a wide area isn't exactly an aimless exercise. Both activities require a high degree of planning and navigation skills.

At the end of the day, hunters and hikers want to make the most of their limited time in the field and still get back home safely when the trip is over. That's why knowing how to use a GPS receiver is important. In this chapter we'll go on a hunting trip with our old pal Crusty to illustrate some key techniques and concepts, including:

- *Navigating on roads and highways—to Crusty's Place*
- *Trip planning and data management with GPS software*
- *Setting up a track log*
- *Navigating an active route*
- *Taking a compass bearing*
- *Backtracking*

Getting to Crusty's Place

The rolling terrain between the foothills of the Adirondack Mountains and the St. Lawrence River plain in upstate New York isn't a hiker's typical destination. There are no dramatic peaks or wide-open vistas of wildflowers; just a lot of low ridges and tumbling streams, timber and marshy bottom-lands—perfect for fishing and hunting. Crusty lives up here in a cabin overgrown with moss and weeds at the end of a dirt road.

I'm taking a couple days off work around the Thanksgiving holiday to go whitetail hunting with Crusty. Not because I want to—I'd rather be sitting in my own tree stand—but because I haven't seen Crusty in a long time and he's getting too old to hunt alone. That's my opinion, anyway. Crusty would disagree.

The plan is to get up to the cabin early so Crusty can show me the lay of the land, locations of tree stands, food plots, deer trails and so on. Along with my hunting gear I pack my GPS receiver, a laptop computer loaded with mapping software and extra aspirin to kill the headache Crusty is sure to give me about hauling all this techno junk to his cabin and running up his power bill.

Navigating in a Whiteout

Late November is a tricky time of year in this region. Snow can start falling in late October and doesn't often melt until mid-April. And heavy, wet snow off Lake Ontario falls by the foot in sudden, unpredictable squalls. One minute it's clear, the next minute everything's white. Yet, conditions can be completely different 5 miles (8 km) away.

That's what happens on the way to Crusty's cabin. I don't have the GPS turned on because I know how to get there, but now I can't see any road signs in the whiteout. I can hardly see past the hood of my truck. Cars have stopped on the highway shoulder to wait out the squall, and there's a jackknifed tractor-trailer in the median.

I pull over, initialize my GPS receiver, and hit a "GoTo" to the waypoint for Crusty's cabin. Then I stick the receiver on the dash-board to a strip of Velcro I use just for this purpose. My GPS receiver has an internal basemap, so I flip to the map page. In the map set-up menu, I reset "map detail" to "low" because I don't want the screen cluttered up with unnecessary information. That way I can see where I am at a glance and still pay full attention to the bad road conditions, knowing I won't accidentally miss my exit.

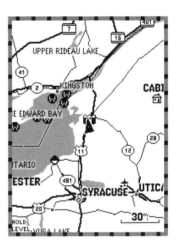

[It's always a good idea to set map details to suit your navigating conditions. For instance, when traveling over large areas at higher speeds (above hiking and trolling speeds), set map detail lower to de-clutter the screen. When navigating in smaller areas at slow speeds, set map details higher to keep track of what's in your immediate vicinity.]

Finding the Cabin

Crusty lives a few miles northeast of the little town of Redfield. The town and the small roads around it aren't on the GPS receiver's basemap, to say nothing about the unmarked turnoff to the dirt road leading to Crusty's cabin. Using the compass page now as a general guide, I head northeast. I probably should have marked the location of the turnoff last night using my GPS mapping software. But at least I have the location of Crusty's cabin stored as a way-point. And thankfully the snow squall has stopped.

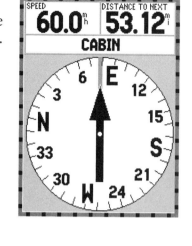

I notice that the compass needle has now swung due east, and the distance reading to my waypoint has started to go up instead of down. I'm moving away from my "GoTo" destination, Crusty's cabin. Darn! Must've missed the turnoff. I turn around and head back, glancing at the compass needle every so often.

I remember that the dirt road to Crusty's cabin heads almost due north from the turnoff. When the compass needle starts to swing back toward north I slow down until I see a small break in the trees: the turnoff! I hit the "Mark" key so I'll have the location saved for next time. After I shift the truck into 4-low, I inch down the dirt road to Crusty's cabin.

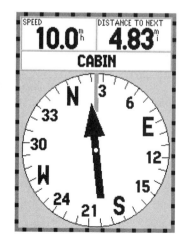

[When navigating backroads, it's not a good idea to use the GPS receiver's digital map as if it were a paper road map. It's not safe, for one thing. Keep your eyes on the road by selecting a "GoTo" desti-nation and use the compass page as a general indicator of the direc-tion you need to go. For instance, if you hit a fork in the road and the compass needle points right, you know that the left fork is probably the wrong direction.]

Trip Planning with GPS

Crusty is in a bad mood when I arrive. There's only a couple of hours of daylight left, he grumbles, not enough time for us to get into the woods and plan our hunting day for tomorrow. I explain that I'm lucky to be here at all and couldn't have done it without my GPS unit. I switch on my laptop computer and pull up a digital version of the Redfield USGS topographic quad map.

Crusty has a dozen different tree stands scattered around nearly 4 square miles (10.4 sq km) of property. The idea is to plot the location of his stands, along with other features such as game trails, buck rubs, bedding areas, mineral licks, food plots and so on. That's what I do for the areas I normally hunt to ensure I'm always in the right place at the right time.

[GPS receivers aren't merely navigation tools; they're also great research and planning tools. Knowing where to find recent game trails, bedding and feeding areas, scrapes and rubs, before opening day means hunters can react intelligently to field conditions, like changes in wind direction.]

[For hikers and campers, knowing beforehand where to find alternative campsites and shelters, trailheads, water sources and ranger stations, means spending less time huddled around maps when field conditions force a change in plans.]

After an hour of scrolling and panning around the digital map while trying to match what's on the screen to Crusty's foggy memory of actual locations in the field, Crusty grumbles and leaves the room. He comes back with a crinkled, old paper quad map, which he rolls out on the kitchen table. His chicken scratches are penciled all over the map, and map details have rubbed off along sharp creases and folds. But it's pretty clear where his tree stands are positioned.

Using the paper quad as a reference, I plot the location of six tree stands on the digital map loaded on my laptop. I also plot some additional locations that might produce whitetails. The software makes this task incredibly easy. With a point and click, I can mark a spot on the digital map and get its exact coordinates.

For instance, there's a swampy plateau bordered by woods on the northern edge of Crusty's property that looks promising (waypoint "Swamp"). And in the southeast corner, a series of

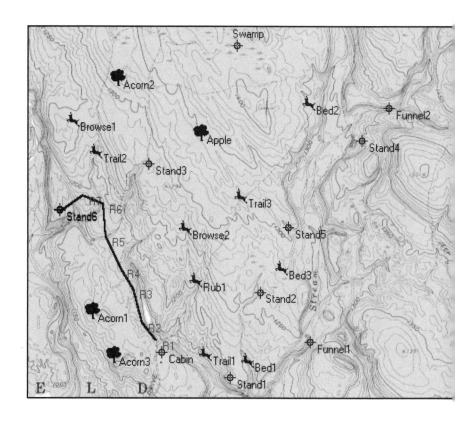

ridges and low bluffs dip toward a stream, a textbook funnel that likely has deer trails running through it (waypoints "Funnel1" and "Funnel2").

[Plotting waypoints and routes from digital or paper maps is convenient, but true backcountry has a way of making a mockery of map details. For instance, swamps and other seasonal land features might appear out of nowhere, and trails that appear clearly on a map can be overgrown or impassable. It's always a good strategy to use plotted waypoints and routes only as a useful reference and correct or replace them in the field.]

When I finish plotting positions on the digital map, I hook up my GPS receiver to the laptop, and with a single keystroke all my waypoints and routes get downloaded into the receiver's memory. I might have arrived too late to get the lay of the land with Crusty, but having the trip planning software available helped salvage a hunting trip from what otherwise would've been an exercise in frustration.

Waypoints From Above

If you're flying in for a hunt, as is often the case in rugged, remote terrain like that in Alaska and northern Canada, take advantage of the bird's-eye view and mark waypoints as you fly over areas of interest, such as lakes big enough to land floatplanes or clearings for helicopters. You'll be glad you did when it comes time to pack game to a pick-up location, and you'll have the confidence to hunt farther from camp.

If you can't get a fix inside the cockpit— or even move your arms in the cramped space—ask for landmark coordinates from bush pilots and guides. They know the terrain better than anybody.

I check the sun/moon calendar in my GPS receiver to see what time I need to wake up. I want to be in my stand before sunrise.

Before going to bed, we go over the plan one more time. From sunrise to midday, Crusty will take Stand1 and I'll take Stand6. At midday, or if conditions force us to move before then, Crusty will try Stand2 and I'll take a new position at Stand3. If one of us gets lucky, we'll know where to find each other. If not, we'll meet back at the cabin at 4:30 p.m., half an hour before sunset.

Setting Up a Track Log

The first thing I do is put new batteries in my GPS receiver and clear the track memory. What's that? In Chapter 1 we discussed how your GPS receiver automatically leaves a "track" or electronic breadcrumb trail that traces your exact steps. You can turn this trail into a route if you need to retrace your steps in the same exact manner in which Hansel and Gretel navigated their way out of the dark forest—by following their breadcrumb trail back home.

Even so, I think it's a good idea to clear your track log memory before setting off on a new trip to ensure you will have enough electronic breadcrumbs. This also helps avoid confusion when you want to turn your track into a route in order to retrace your steps.

Track logs, like loaves of bread, are not permanent, however. You don't have an unlimited number of electronic breadcrumbs. When the GPS receiver runs out of points to draw your trail, it starts erasing them from the beginning and adding them to the end.

Since I used my GPS receiver on the drive up to Crusty's I probably wasted a lot of track points. Clearing the track memory will ensure that I have enough track points to trace my steps on the hunt. In the event I want to create a route and retrace my steps, the route won't include track points that were laid down miles away during the drive up to Crusty's.

Another thing I want to do is set the interval at which the GPS receiver drops electronic breadcrumbs to 3 feet (1 m). That means pretty much every step I take will be recorded automatically.

Short track-point intervals are best when hiking over relatively small areas, and result in high-resolution track logs that show your every twist and turn.

Long track-point intervals are best when driving or covering large distances on well-marked routes, such as a desert highway in Nevada.

Trailblazer

If you discover an unmarked trail, whether it's a hiking trail or game trail, don't just hit the "Mark" key—actually walk the trail as far as you can. Make sure your GPS receiver has a good position fix, and that your track log is set up to drop electronic bread-crumbs more frequently. Save the track log and, when you get home, download it to your computer.

If you have digital mapping software, you can overlay your track log on the map contours and create a permanent new trail that only exists on your own maps.

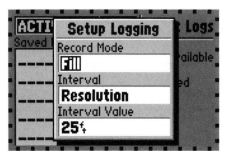

This is the submenu of a track log setup page showing choices for recording track points.

Navigating an Active Route

Last night I created a route to Stand6 because I don't know the area well. Why not go straight to it using a "GoTo"? Why navigate a route? Isn't this overkill? That might be true if I were navigating an empty parking lot. But as we know, the straightest route to your destination in the backcountry is never a straight line. I'll be in the dark, and I'd rather not spread my scent or make any more noise than I have to.

As Crusty sets off in one direction to Stand6, I activate the route and get a bearing to the first waypoint. The GPS receiver gets stowed in my breast pocket so the antenna has at least a partial view of the sky at all times. The route is a little over a mile (1.6 km) long, and every few minutes I take a new bearing to the next leg.

If I were navigating straight to Stand6, I probably would've made a few false starts in directions that seemed promising at first, only to be turned around by thick tangles of

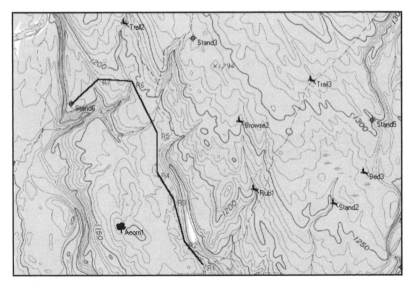

thorny scrub. The way I planned it, each leg of my route will keep me on relatively flat terrain, along the lip of a low ridge so I can I keep my footing and move as quickly as possible to Stand6.

The sky is turning pink and purple in the east by the time I reach Stand6. I situate myself and switch off the GPS receiver to conserve battery life. A warm wind is blowing from a south-westerly direction. For the moment, I'm downwind from the deer trail Crusty had marked on his paper map, which I now have stored in my GPS receiver as waypoint Trail2, just north of my position. The map page shows all the other way-points as well, how far each is from my tree stand, and their bearing. If I need to leave this position, I have a dozen others at the ready.

```
┌─────────────────────────┐
│         Route           │
├─────────────────────────┤
│ STAND6-STAND3           │
├─────────────────────────┤
│ Waypoint     ◄ Distance ►│
│ STAND6         0.00ᶠᵗ   │
│ TRAIL2         1.28ᵐⁱ   │
│ STAND3         3.01ᵐⁱ   │
│ ────────────   ──+──ᵐⁱ  │
│                         │
├─────────────────────────┤
│ Total          3.01ᵐⁱ   │
└─────────────────────────┘
```

As dawn brightens into day, I notice a candy wrapper stuck in the crotch of the tree, and scattered on the ground below me are cigarette butts and a crumpled package of ciga-rettes—not Crusty's brand, either. Some other jerk has been using this stand, probably in the last couple of days.

Favorable wind or not, this area is contaminated. No doubt the deer have been avoiding it. This is just the kind of annoying thing that no amount of careful trip planning could've helped. Guess I'll have to go to Plan B and try Stand3.

I turn on the GPS receiver and call up the position for Stand3, but instead of hitting "GoTo," I create a short route. Before heading straight to Stand3, I want to check out the nearby deer trail (waypoint Trail2) to see if there's been any recent activity.

Of course, I could simply "GoTo" Trail2, then punch in a new "GoTo" for Stand3 once I get there. But I'd rather do all of my button pushing right here in a spot where I know I'm not going to scare game away by lingering too long near trails and bedding areas.

Don't Pass the Buck

Old bucks get old because they've learned to stay out of sight. That makes it all the more important to mark locations where you see these big boys, even if you only catch a glimpse of one crossing the road or waving his flag at you 200 yards (182 m) away before disappearing into the tree line. For instance, if you see a particular buck ten times over three years, and you happened to mark each location with your GPS receiver, you might see a pattern begin to emerge that reveals his otherwise-secret ranging habits.

I go to the route page and create two legs out of existing waypoints from the database: one leg for getting me to Trail2, and the other linking Trail2 to Stand3.

Sure enough, when I get there, Trail2 is cold as stone. There are deer tracks all right, but they're at least a day old because snow has blown into some of them and the carpet of wet, dead leaves shows no signs of being disturbed. I take a quick bearing to Stand3 from the GPS receiver and head in that direction.

At the top of the hill I pause at a tree line and scan the scrubby meadow before me. In the far corner of the meadow I see the grayish brown flank of a whitetail against the dark backdrop of pine trees. Through my binoculars I see that it's a doe accompanied by two fawns almost hidden by the high brush. I glance at my GPS receiver and note that I'm about a quarter mile (0.4 km) north of Stand3, which means the deer might be moving out of the low areas to browse on the plateau.

Stand3 overlooks a steep trail that comes out of a ravine and continues on toward the plateau. The wind has shifted, coming out of the north now. It's cold and dry and, unfortunately, blowing my scent right down the trail. I shiver in the stand for a couple of hours and see nothing.

I'm faced with the typical hunter's dilemma: Should I stay or should I go? A wise, patient hunter would remain in the stand and wait. But I'm curious to see if my theory about deer moving from the low areas to higher areas is correct. Plus, I need to warm up; a walk would help.

Changing the Plan

Turns out Crusty didn't have any luck either. We didn't come home empty-handed, though. We have real field intelligence to help us plan tomorrow's hunt. I hook up my GPS receiver to the laptop computer and download my track log and any new waypoints I marked earlier that day. With the mapping software I can view my exact path throughout the day plotted right on the digital topographic map along with new waypoint locations. I point to the screen and explain my theory of deer movement to Crusty.

"I think the deer are running northeast, up onto the plateau," I say. "You know that old apple orchard up there, I think maybe—"

"Got nothing to do with apples," Crusty says with a dismissive wave of his gnarled hand. "If they're moving the way you say they are, they're getting away from them damn fools hunting down by the road. I saw trucks parked along that road all week."

That would explain the cigarette butts around my tree stand. I trace my track log on the screen. Earlier that day, after I'd abandoned Stand3, I scouted the swamp. It was almost completely surrounded by pine trees, which I marked to give me a sense of the swamp's borders on the digital map. The dense

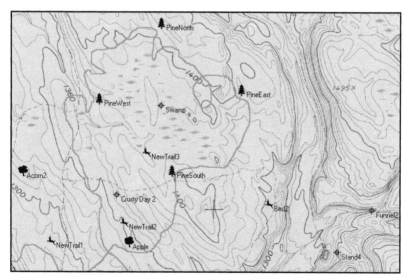

This track log (the dotted line) is a record of our morning activities.

branches and beds of pine needles offer ideal protection for spooked deer. It was all starting to make perfect sense now.

"They could be taking cover in the swamp," I say.

Crusty scratches his grizzled chin. "Could be right," he says. "Could be right."

Coming from Crusty, that's a compliment. While he fries up some venison steaks, I plot a new route on the digital map, along with alternative stand sites. Then I download everything to my GPS receiver and switch on the radio to get the weather forecast. Twenty-six degrees, getting colder through the day. Sixty-percent chance of snow squalls. Good hunting conditions.

[On this outing, I learned one lesson well: Trip planning might begin at home, but it doesn't end there. Always supplement your maps, routes and waypoints with up-to-date field intelligence. Likewise, delete old waypoints, routes and track logs to keep maps—digital and paper—fresh.]

In the brittle, cold dark the next morning I navigate a route I'd downloaded into the GPS receiver that skirts alongside a creek bed to my destination, "Stand 4." Crusty heads off toward a new location, "CrustyDay2," which I'd scouted yesterday on a trail between the swamp and the old apple orchard.

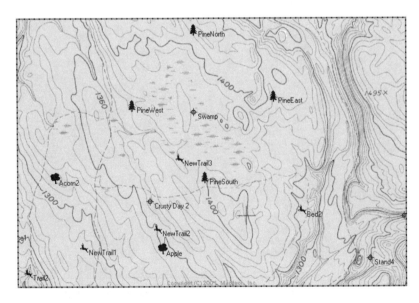

The plan calls for Crusty to remain there all day while I push the low areas along the creek, kicking up any deer bedding in the protection of the many hollows and ravines on the western edge of his property. If my theory is right, the deer should take off northwest over the plateau and into the swamp, right past Crusty.

Taking a Compass Bearing

Around 2 p.m. a gunshot echoes through the trees. That has to be Crusty! I pull out my GPS receiver but I can't get a position fix. The steep slopes of the ravine I'm standing in are blocking the satellite signals. Scrambling up the ravine, I lose my footing in a hole hidden by loose leaves and drop the GPS receiver. It cracks against an icy rock. The screen goes as blank as the gunmetal-gray sky above me. The battery compartment cover is missing along with the batteries. I don't know if the GPS receiver is permanently damaged or not, but I can't afford to waste time pawing through snow and leaves looking for batteries.

At the top of the ravine I pull out my compass. Although I don't have a map, I know I must be somewhere east of the trail Crusty took to get to CrustyDay2 this morning.

If I head due west I should intersect his trail. I rest my gun against a sapling—I don't want any metal near the compass needle—and hold the compass level above my waist. Then I rotate the azimuth ring until the West cardinal heading (270°) lines up with the direction-of-travel arrow. Slowly I turn my body, keeping the compass level and stationary until the red end of the magnetic needle lines up with the orienting arrow.

With the bearing now set, I look up and see a large oak tree across the meadow that falls on a line due west of my position. When I get to the oak tree, I take another bearing due west toward a tall pine tree on a knoll. Halfway to the pine tree I come across Crusty's tracks in the thin layer of ice and snow covering the trail.

Backtracking

By the time I reach the cabin it's beginning to snow. There's only about an hour of daylight left. Hunting through the utility drawer in Crusty's kitchen, I find the GPS receiver that Crusty's children bought for him and power it up. It works! Duct tape keeps it stuck to the handlebars of Crusty's ATV as I take off north through the blowing snow toward the swamp.

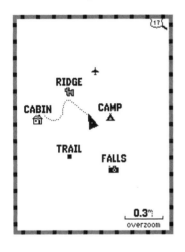

I find Crusty waiting patiently in the fringe of pine trees that surround the swamp. At his feet is an eight-pointer that must dress out at around 175 pounds (80 kg). The trail I took to get here is already covered in fresh snow. And we can't leave the buck until morning or the coyotes, foxes and crows will have a field day with it.

I check Crusty's GPS receiver. There are a few unknown waypoints on the plotter page. But I don't need them to navigate by because there's a complete track log of my path from the cabin to our current position.

We can easily retrace my path because Crusty's GPS receiver, like most GPS receivers, has a "backtrack" feature that allows me to turn the track log into a route. I activate the backtrack feature in the setup menu. The GPS receiver automatically calculates a series of waypoints linking our position to the cabin, using the track log as its line of reference.

It's dark when we finally get the buck tied onto the ATV. Trouble is, there's only room for one of us. "Why don't you head back on the ATV," I tell Crusty. "Age before beauty."

Crusty squints at the GPS receiver duct-taped to the handlebars. He leans close to the screen, confused by what he sees. Then he looks around the darkened woods to get his bearings. Snow swirls in the ATV's dim headlight beam.

"I can walk back, dammit," he says.

"Crusty, it's miles away," I say. "And it's all blow-downs and frozen marsh. It'll be hours before—"

"Look here," Crusty says, pointing his finger at me. "I can walk outta here blindfolded and get back in half the time it'd take you."

I try another approach that won't challenge Crusty's enormous pride. Skipping to the GPS receiver's compass page, I show him the arrow pointing to the first waypoint on the route. I explain that all he has to do is follow the direction of the arrow. No fiddling with buttons or submenus or anything at all. It's got a backlight so he can see the screen in the dark. Even Crusty can't begrudge the GPS receiver's ability to navigate under these conditions with virtually no input.

"Well ain't that something," he says.

"The way I look at it, you've got the hard part," I tell him. "I'll just follow your trail on foot. But if you want, I can try to make it back to the cabin on the ATV. I mean, if I don't roll it down a ravine first and lose your nice buck here."

"And let me starve all winter?"

"It's up to you, Crusty."

My track log has become a backtrack route, and is now highlighted.

"No thanks!" Pride intact, Crusty climbs on the ATV and pops it into gear. The headlight beam bobs through the dark. When it disappears I start trudging back toward the cabin.

CHAPTER 6

Fishing or Boating with GPS

From their inception GPS receivers have been extremely popular with aviators and mariners. Every radio-navigation technology that has come along in the past sixty years, such as radar, sonar, LORAN, microwave, has been applied toward the goal of making it easier, safer and more efficient to get ships and planes to their destinations. GPS has revolutionized and, in some cases, replaced these technologies. It's easy to see why. In the air and on the water, where an open view of the sky is never a problem, GPS satellite signals are always available, and their range isn't limited to the nearest radar station or LORAN transmitter.

Catching fish isn't about technology. It's not about the color of your lure or the cost of your boat, either. It's about being in the right place at the right time, just as hunting is about being where the game is. And that's what a GPS receiver does best. It can't tell you where the fish are, of course, but it will guide you safely to the exact spot where you landed that lunker in the weeds two years ago.

In general the navigation techniques described in Chapter 5 apply equally to marine navigation. In this chapter we'll discuss some important differences between navigating on land and navigating on water, including tips on:

- *Marking, naming and finding your favorite fishing holes*
- *Using a track log as a fishing tool*
- *Fishing maps versus NOAA charts*
- *Assigning waypoint nametags*
- *Determining whether a GPS receiver is "waterproof"*

Land Versus Water

Getting from Point A to Point B on open water has all the pit-falls of land navigation with none of the advantages. As we already know, navigating a "GoTo" straight to a backcountry destination rarely occurs in a straight line. But at least the hiker or hunter can usually see the "structure" that separates them from their intended destination.

For instance, mountain climbers can see the sheer cliff face between themselves and the mountain peak they're trying to reach. And they can plan a route around it, whether at home using special digital mapping software or right there on the spot.

On the water, however, there are precious few landmarks. And in some situations, such as offshore boating or sport fishing on a large lake out of view of the shoreline, there are no land-marks whatsoever. All the "structure" is underwater.

With land navigation, there's little danger in inadvertently run-ning into obstacles. They're usually visible from a distance. Even if you're particularly klutzy and still manage to collide with a landmark—say, a tree—the potential for harm is quite limited.

The opposite applies to marine navigation. If you're zipping across a lake in a boat, the obstacles that matter—shoals, rocks, sandbars—are hidden from view, and you learn about them only after you bang a prop, or worse, punch a hole in your hull.

Learn the Lingo

GPS receivers, even those sold specifically for marine use, still reflect the bias of the landlubbers who made them. Power it up, what do you see? Miles per hour or knots? Is it set for statute miles (on land) or nautical miles (1.2 statute miles)? How about the coordinate system? Latitude and longitude, right? Great, at least they got that right—or did they? No, the coordinates are set for degrees/minutes/decimal minutes, not the properly nautical degrees/minutes/seconds. It's enough to make an old salt cry in his grog.

Does it matter? Not unless you're working with other sources, such as paper sea charts, that display all navigation data in nautical terms. If you insist on the full marine experience, your GPS receiver's distance, speed and position measurements can be reset for knots, nautical miles and degrees/minutes/seconds. And the map display can be "reversed" for use on water, making it easier to read in bright sunlight. You don't have to be an old salty dog to appreciate that.

The potential for harm is dramatic. There's no such thing as a small accident in a boat.

Further complicating matters, land navigation is all about avoiding or going around obstacles to reach a chosen destination. But an obstacle or "structure" is often the angler's intended destination, not something to avoid. Shoals, shallow areas, rocks, submerged logs and so on, often shelter fish. Knowing how to use your GPS receiver (especially the route creation and navigation features) is critically important when navigating open water, whether it's a lake, river, mangrove swamp or ocean. If you remember the following principles, only your bait will get wet!

Marking Waypoints

Marking the location of a favorite fishing hole is the best use of a GPS receiver. If you have a depth sounder mounted on your console, you don't need me to tell you that it's a good idea to mark underwater structure where fish take cover such as:

• *Standing timber*

• *Weed beds*

• *Ledges*

• *Creek channels*

• *Submerged roadbeds, fencerows or any other structure familiar to reservoirs or other manmade bodies of water*

• *Rock piles*

• *Bottom types, such as mud, gravel and sand*

Even if you're not an avid angler and just enjoy cruising on a hot day, you'll want to mark locations such as:

• *Boating and shipping lanes*

• *Shoals*

• *Breakwaters*

• *Access roads*

• *Marker buoys*

• *Hazards*

• *Land features such as lighthouses, marinas and swimming areas*

It's not enough, however, for the boater and angler to simply hit the "Mark" key in the same way that a hiker or hunter saves the location of a trailhead. Why? A location is a location, right? Yes, but on water you're constantly moving, even if it doesn't seem like it.

If you cut the motor in a protected bay to cast into weeds for large-mouth bass, you're still moving. Wind, currents and wave action will always push your hull one way or another. Throwing an anchor overboard might keep you in one spot but, depending on the conditions, you're going to swing in a circle around the anchor.

So, marking waypoints on the water is complicated by the fact you are always moving, as opposed to marking static waypoints on land.

Position Averaging

Many GPS receivers offer you the choice of "position averaging" when you mark a location. This is a great idea for land navigation, but it doesn't make much sense for marine navigation. Here's why:

When your GPS receiver averages a position, it is taking many waypoints in a short burst of time, requiring you to stand still until it's finished. It then samples an average to come up with a more precise position.

But remember, on the water you're always moving. If you use position averaging to mark a fishing hole, the area sampled by your GPS receiver includes the area covered by your drift. The sample area will be greatly increased, and your waypoint will be less precise, not more.

Finding a Fishing Spot

Here's one of my personal examples of the most basic task an angler or boater might perform with his or her GPS receiver: I'm in the middle of the St. Lawrence River on the border between Canada and northern New York. The lower section of the St. Lawrence River near Lake Ontario is renowned for its feisty black bass, a species of smallmouth. It's a breezy summer day and I've got a shiner cast overboard at a depth of about 40 feet (12 m). Suddenly the tip of my rod bends…

[This is the precise moment I should hit the "Mark" key on my GPS receiver, right? After all, this is the exact spot where I caught the fish. So this is the spot I'll want to come back to later. But am I really going to set the rod down while I hunt around for my GPS receiver, mark the spot, and try to come up with a name for the waypoint? Not a chance. I came here to fish, not play with electronic gadgets.]

…And I give the rod a yank to set the hook and start reeling. I can tell it's a good-size smallmouth, a real fighter. I don't want to lose it, so I loosen the drag a little to tire it out. The line cuts the water back and forth and the reel squeals as the small-mouth rips off some line. I reel up the slack and pause to let the fish tear off some more. Pretty soon it starts to tire, and I can reel it straight in.

At the surface the fish spooks and tries to run again, taking off more line. I reel it up quickly and the bass comes to the boat slapping and leaping out of the water. I net it and work the hook from its mouth. It's a beautiful monster; I better get the tape measure out. I fumble around in the tackle box looking for the tape measure. A hair over 17 inches (43 cm)! A new record for me. After I finally find my camera and snap some pictures, I return the smallmouth to the river. In a flash of bronze it darts back into the depths.

So, about ten or fifteen minutes after the smallmouth bent the tip of my rod I finally get around to marking a GPS waypoint. In the meantime the boat has been slowly, consistently, drifting downriver. Not fast enough for me to notice or worry about hitting an obstacle, but drifting all the same.

If I had drifted even at the measly rate of 1 mph (1.6 kmph) due to river current and wind, in fifteen minutes I would've moved a quarter mile (0.4 km) from the exact location where I hooked the smallmouth. Add to that distance some 50 feet (15 m) of fishing line that I had reeled out, plus the average position error of the GPS receiver of 49 feet (15 meters), and the grand total adds up to more than 1,400 feet (427 m)!

Any experienced angler knows that if you're off the fish by 30 feet (9 m), you might as well be off by 30 miles (48 km).

If I returned to that same waypoint later that day, or the next week, or the next year for that matter, I'd be 1,400 feet (427 m) off the location that I really want. I shouldn't be surprised if I get skunked.

Okay, maybe my example was a bit extreme. Let's say I somehow managed to mark the position only six minutes after I hooked the smallmouth, my drift rate was only 0.5 mph (0.8 kmph), and I had only 15 feet (4.5 m) of fishing line reeled out. That's still leaves me 328 feet (100 m) off the point where the smallmouth took the bait. If the best position error achievable by GPS receivers was 328 feet—to say nothing about 1,400 feet—few people would buy them.

So, should you give up on marking waypoints on the water? Of course not. What good would your GPS receiver be if you couldn't accurately navigate to your favorite fishing spots? You only have to learn a few simple, common-sense techniques.

Triangulate Your Position

If you get a strike or some nibbles, or maybe you're cruising past a promising location that you want to return to later when the fish are biting, try to sight onshore landmarks. These can include buildings, docks, rock formations, trees, creek channels, cattails and bulrushes, navigational buoys or lights—anything that will jog your memory.

On water you use triangulation exactly as you'd use it on land to get your bearings with a compass. Coupled with a saved waypoint, you'll have a much better chance of getting back to a productive spot.

But what if you're fishing featureless lakes or reservoirs without distinct shoreline landmarks or islands? Or you're carving a watery trail through mangrove that all looks the

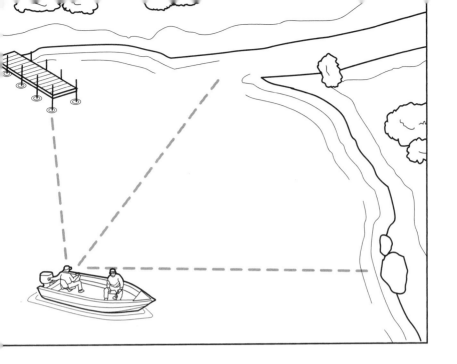

same? Having a precise waypoint to navigate toward is even more important. Here are three other techniques to try.

Mark a "Hole"

This is really a shotgun approach to marking waypoints, and it works because the term "fishing hole" is not quite accurate in the first place. Remember, fish don't live in holes, they move from structure to structure in search of food or mates, or to escape predators.

These structures tend to be large objects that offer cover, or natural features that don't have distinct edges. Fish can be found all around these structures and features depending upon conditions, so you don't want to be fishing the exact same spot every time anyway.

If you catch a bass in one spot, chances are pretty good that there are more bass in the area. Bass are no different than anglers—they return again and again to productive areas where there's food. Trace the lip of a long ledge or a drop-off and mark waypoints in more than one place. Likewise, use multiple waypoints to define an area, such as an entire weed bed, as opposed to an arbitrary fixed location somewhere in the middle of the weed bed.

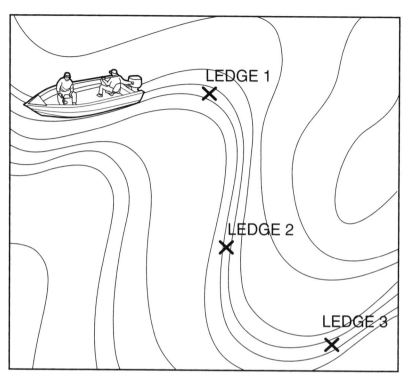

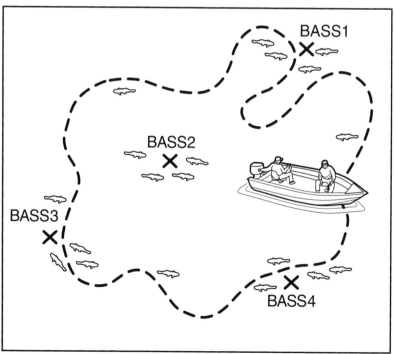

Use MOB

Some years ago most GPS receivers were sold with a dedicated key labeled "MOB" (Man Over Board). How was using the MOB key different than marking a waypoint? When you activated your receiver's MOB function, it didn't force you through the tedious process of naming the waypoint, picking an icon, etc. It instantly saved your position coordinates and jumped to a new page that took you back to those coordinates. The idea was that if someone fell overboard from a moving vessel, another person could hit the MOB key and immediately begin navigating to the spot as the vessel swung around to pick up the wet soul.

These days, only specialized marine units have an MOB key, but many GPS receivers still retain the MOB function. Check your manual to learn how to activate it. Usually it requires something simple, such as hitting the "Mark" or "GoTo" key twice in a row.

After you reel in the fish you can change the name of the MOB, and your coordinates will be much closer to where you hooked the fish than saving a waypoint using the conventional method.

Use a Track Log

If you forgot to save a waypoint where you caught a mess of fish, that doesn't mean there's no record of where you caught them. Track logs—those electronic breadcrumb trails—provide an excellent source of precision waypoints, but it requires timely attention.

Most anglers zip from one fishing spot to another; or they troll along a feature such as a steep ledge, turn around, and troll back over the same ledge. In both cases, their track log will show straight lines that suddenly shift or change direction as they settle into a new fishing hole or trolling run.

If you started hitting fish at the beginning or middle of a trolling run, move the cursor over that particular spot on the track log and mark a waypoint. Or if you get a bite twenty minutes after locating a new fishing hole, try to pinpoint that part of the track log, keeping in mind that track points are dropped at regular intervals of either time or distance (you can check or change these intervals in the track log setup menu).

Zoom in to maximum resolution and count the track points based on your best estimate of where you caught the first fish, starting from the track point where you began drifting or using the trolling motor.

Waypoints taken from a track log can be more accurate than waypoints saved using the conventional method because you were actually floating over the spot indicated by a single track point, not drifting beyond it.

The Weather Factor

Most of us seldom leave our home waters. That means we're pretty comfortable zipping across a lake. We know where all the danger areas and fishing holes are located, so hitting a "GoTo" on our GPS receivers is as complicated as marine navigation gets for us.

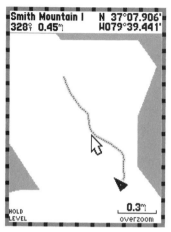

Here's a track log of a trolling run.

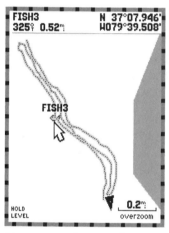

You can mark waypoints right from your track log by moving the cursor arrow over a certain spot.

So why go through the trouble of building routes? Using a saved route is the best way to navigate under less-than-ideal conditions.

Until you can predict the weather at any given moment with 100% accuracy, it's a good idea to keep at least one or two routes saved in your GPS receiver's database. Here's an example of how it helped me:

Oneida Lake in upstate New York is one of the best walleye lakes in the country. It's relatively shallow, so it doesn't take much wind to get a good chop going. When I'm jigging for walleyes off a sandbar in the middle of the lake, a little chop can be handy. But when a thunderstorm blows in, I prefer to yank the cord and head back for the marina before the lake has a chance to turn into a raging sea. But I'm not always fast enough.

One hot summer day I was trying my luck with smallmouth bass in a sheltered cove. All afternoon dark clouds had been gathering and pressing down on the horizon. But the fishing was fantastic! Half the time I was getting contact strikes before the lure had a chance to sink just below the waves. It had more to do with the dropping air pressure than my angling skills, so I didn't want to give it up quite so soon. When I felt the first blast of cool wind I decided to get out of there. I didn't stop to consider that conditions in the cove, which was somewhat protected, would be smoother than on the lake itself. As soon as I left the cove I hit the chop.

My little aluminum 14-footer (4-m) bounced over the whitecaps. I turned on my GPS receiver to see how far it was to the marina. Six miles (10 m). A quick check of the POI database showed the nearest marina at about the same distance away, so I decided to head to the one where I was parked. What difference would it make? A lot, it turned out. As soon as I came around the tip of the island separating me from the last straight run to the marina the chop turned into serious waves.

Suddenly, the bow banged into a trough, overturning my tackle box and spilling gear everywhere. I had to corner the boat into the waves to keep from getting swamped, and soon I was way off course. It was hard to tell exactly where I was with all the bouncing and rolling. At this point, I started to worry whether the local news report was going to spell my name right after my body washed ashore.

And then the rain started. I say "rain" but this didn't classify as rain. It was a solid sheet of water that blurred the horizon and instantly soaked everything it touched. Now I was truly worried. Lightning crackled and thunder boomed.

In four quick keystrokes (Menu to Routes to Saved Routes to Enter) I punched up a GPS route that I keep saved in my database for these kinds of emergency situations. It's a short route with two legs leading from a safe point in the lake ("Point"), approachable from any direction, about 1 mile (0.9 m) from the marina ("Ramp"). The route then makes a turn past a concrete breakwater, and finally turns again into the marina.

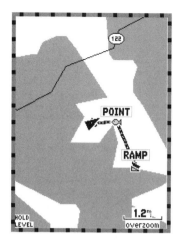

It took me another twenty minutes of slamming and steering and praying every time a lightning bolt struck the shoreline, but I got back to the marina. Sure, I might have returned to the marina without the GPS receiver. I might have made it back without the boat, too, or my fishing gear. It'd all be sitting at the bottom of Oneida Lake while I doggy-paddled to shore.

One thing is for certain, without the saved route at the ready, the GPS receiver wouldn't have done me much good—not under those conditions. With visibility down to a few feet, I could've easily hit the concrete breakwater, among other things.

It's easy to get lulled into the habit of pressing "GoTo" every time. My advice? Have a backup plan for the times when straight-line navigation isn't going to cut it.

Fishing Maps

Detailed mapping of most inland freshwater lakes and rivers has been left to private companies. You can buy paper or digital "fishing maps" that allow you to take GPS coordinates directly from the map in the same way you learned to enter GPS coordinates from USGS topographic maps in Chapter 4.

How are fishing maps different than the preloaded basemaps that come with GPS receivers? Your basemap is generalized and permanent, and it lacks any significant detail of lakes and rivers.

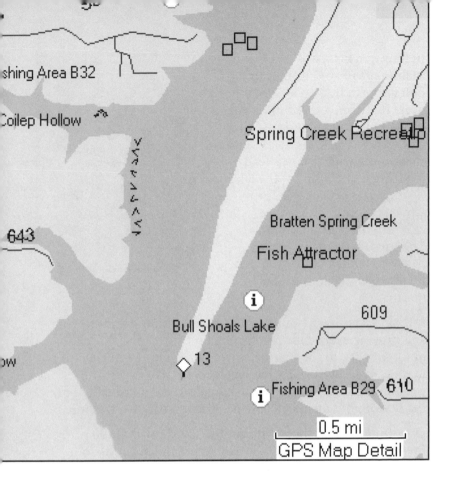

shing Area B32

Coilep Hollow

Spring Creek Recreati

Bratten Spring Creek

Fish Attractor

643

ⓘ

Bull Shoals Lake

609

◇ 13

ow

ⓘ Fishing Area B29 610

0.5 mi

GPS Map Detail

Are fishing maps the same thing as the "marine" software sold by the same company that makes your GPS receiver? Yes and no. There might be overlap of certain information, like shoreline details, depth contours and locations of navigational aids, but separate "marine" or "nautical" databases and software are usually designed with the boater in mind.

So what the heck is a fishing map, and why would I want one? Fishing maps are specially designed to aid the angler by giving the GPS coordinates of underwater structure that will help find fish on unfamiliar lakes and rivers. This information requires a lot of memory, so electronic fishing maps must be downloaded by specific region. Fishing maps also contain other useful information about seasonal changes in underwater topography and special tips for fishing various species.

Remember that no electronic map makes any promises. At best it can point you in the right direction and keep you from wasting your time running lines in unproductive areas. You still have to find the fish!

Last but not least, trading waypoints with a trusted fishing buddy is a great way to build your database of fishing holes. Just make sure you get a fair trade, waypoint for waypoint, lunker for lunker, and that your map datums match.

NOAA Charts

National Oceanic and Atmospheric Administration (NOAA) charts are to marine navigation what USGS topographic maps are to land navigation. They cover in fine detail all U.S. coastal areas, including Alaska and Hawaii, from the shoreline to the continental shelf. Only the most heavily traveled freshwater lakes and rivers are mapped in similar detail. Offshore and blue-water boaters use both paper charts and electronic cartridges that plug into chartplotters.

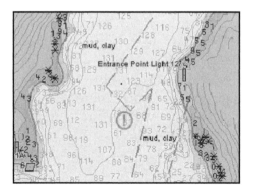

The Rap on Fishing Maps

Fishing maps, both paper and electronic, provide an excellent source of detailed information about uncharted freshwater lakes and rivers, including depth contours and GPS coordinates of underwater structure. But how accurate are they?

Because most of the time private companies are collecting and applying the data that ends up on the map, there are no hard-and-fast government regulations about accuracy. That doesn't mean fishing maps aren't accurate; it just means their accuracy cannot be easily determined.

The best policy when using fishing maps (or any map for that matter) to navigate unfamiliar waters is to use them only as a general reference. Update the maps with real field intelligence gathered from your own GPS receiver and depth sounder.

NOAA is constantly at work updating the location of navigation aids, resurveying bottom structure and shoreline features, and otherwise improving the accuracy and dependability of sea charts. Check your "local notice to mariners" regularly issued by the Coast Guard, and update your sea charts on a regular basis to get the safety and accuracy benefits of these improvements.

Budget your error...

As good as NOAA charts certainly are, they're prone to the same sources of error and inaccuracies that are inherent to USGS topographic maps. Accuracy depends on the chart's scale and the technology used in gathering field data.

To gauge the accuracy of a particular NOAA chart, divide the chart's scale by 1,000 meters (3,280 feet/.6 mile). A 1:40,000-scale NOAA chart divided by 1,000 meters equals an accuracy range of 40 meters (131 feet). The accuracy of a more detailed 1:10,000-scale chart is 10 meters (33 feet), and so on.

Remember how we added up the error budget for USGS topographic maps in Chapter 4? Let's try it with an NOAA chart.

Since GPS receivers are accurate to within 15 meters (49 feet), your 1:40,000-scale chart is accurate to within 40 meters (131 feet). Your total error budget, then, is 55 meters (180 feet).

No big deal if you're traveling on land, right? You can see almost any obstacle from 55 meters (180 feet/60 yards) away. But that's a hair's-breadth if you're at the helm of a boat navigating treacherous waters. To be safe, always double or triple your error budget for marine navigation.

...and don't forget the datum!

When navigating with an NOAA chart and GPS receiver, don't forget to match the datum listed in the chart's legend. Most sea charts use the NAD-83 datum, which is equivalent to WGS-84 in North America, the same datum that your GPS receiver uses as a default. Double-check to be certain.

Remember: On a boat there's no such thing as a small accident as a result of a minor navigational error.

Waypoint Nametags

At this point in the book you should be comfortable with the simple process of naming waypoints, and you may already be an expert at it. Naming waypoints for marine navigation just takes a little more thought than naming waypoints on land.

You won't always have the time or patience to come up with creative names for the hundreds of waypoints that will accumulate in your GPS receiver's database like dust bunnies under a bed. Having a system that makes sense to you is the key to finding not only specific waypoints, but also the kind of waypoint it is. For instance, when fishing, I always name fishing holes beginning with the letter "Z" and tag each one with a fish icon. So, a typical waypoint in my database might look like "ZBASS," or "ZPERCH3."

If you consider the fact that GPS receivers store waypoints alphabetically (you can also search for waypoints by proximity), my system should start to make sense. When I scroll through my GPS receiver's database, I know that anything beginning with "Z" is a fishing hole, and I find it convenient to have all of my fishing hole locations listed next to each other.

For danger areas, such as shoals, I always begin with the letter "X" and tag each one with a skull icon. A typical danger waypoint looks like "XSHOAL" or "XROCK." When I'm motoring from one waypoint to another, I know at a glance whether I should steer clear of a waypoint or try to land right on it.

Let's say I've worn out one fishing spot and I want to go to another one across the lake, a submerged rock pile with the waypoint name "ROCK8." About 50 feet (15 m) away from "ROCK8" is a boulder 6 inches (15 cm) below the surface that will scrape the lower unit off my boat like a barnacle knife if I happen to hit it. Its name is "ROCK." I'm in a hurry to get to "ROCK8" because the day is

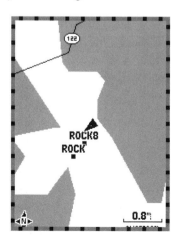

125

starting to heat up and the fishing are moving into deeper water. The throttle is wide open. A glance at my GPS receiver's map page looks like the illustration on page 125.

On land the difference between these two waypoints would be easy to comprehend. I could see them, live and in color. And if I were unsure which was which, I could always stop to figure it out.

Cruising along at 20 knots, however, I could easily mistake the boulder for the rock pile that I actually want to fish because both are hidden underwater.

On the map page they look virtually the same, and they're close to each other. I can throttle back long enough to figure out which waypoint is which, but I can't stop. On the other hand, if I've been consistent with my naming system, I could tell at a glance to steer clear of any waypoints marked "XROCK" because X always means danger.

You can also set up your receiver's map page to display only icons, only names, or both at the same time. Whatever makes it easier for you to separate one waypoint from another. Naming waypoints isn't brain surgery, but having a commonsense system will save you from a little frustration, and potentially big problems down the road.

Water Goof

Some GPS manufacturers claim that their GPS receivers float. It's hard to fake that claim. Something either floats or it doesn't. You might want to contact the GPS manufacturer to ask how long a particular model floats. For a day? An hour? Three minutes? Under what conditions? Hurricane? Calm water? Basically, a GPS receiver that can float will do so long enough for you to turn the boat around and retrieve it.

If your GPS receiver is the sinking kind, as most of them are, get in the habit of using the lanyard strap that came with it. You can also buy a plastic mount to keep it from banging around the boat on a choppy day, or from sliding out of your shirt pocket into the drink.

I know a guy who cuts up those fluorescent foam beverage coolies and wraps them around everything not bolted to the deck, including his GPS receiver. It makes for a rather interesting decorating style, but his GPS receiver stays dry!

Again, there is some lingo to learn: Is your GPS receiver waterproof? Are you sure? Or is it merely water resistant? No, wait, the clerk said weatherproof. Or was that splashproof? Maybe it was weather resistant.

Never mind; most of us get confused by all the marketing jargon anyway. The most important questions are: Can you fully immerse your GPS receiver in water? For how long? At what depth? If you can answer confidently, then you did your homework.

If you're taking your GPS receiver on the water, you better know whether it floats, if it'll survive an accidental dunking, or if a little splash is going to fry the chipboard. If a GPS receiver is advertised as "waterproof," your first question should be: According to what standard?

If your GPS receiver has a rating of IEC 529/ IPX7 or JIS-7, it's dunkable. Equipment rated CFR-46 cannot be immersed. Equipment rated MIL-STD 810 without specific reference to a specific test does not guarantee it can survive a dunking. The NEMA system isn't used much for GPS units but you may see a reference to it.

In the Appendix at the back of the book, the chart called "International Waterproof Ratings" lists the most common standards that you will see advertised, along with abbreviated definitions, which usually are not advertised. These waterproof ratings are a good way to verify exactly how good your unit is, when it comes to getting dunked!

CHAPTER 7

Digital Maps and Software

GPS technology hasn't changed all that much since the first handheld receivers came on the market over twenty years ago. Sure, they're much smaller, and they cost a lot less, but the technology itself is the same. Satellites still broadcast the same radio signals, and the receivers still do the same calculations to figure out where you are. Everyone knows that GPS is great at telling you where you are, but if you want to navigate to a place you've never been, it can't help you—not without a map, anyway. And today's sophisticated mapping receivers are to yesterday's plain-vanilla GPS receivers what high-definition color televisions are to the bulky radio sets of the 1920s.

The shift to digital mapping started just a few years ago, when the first affordable handheld receivers with basemaps hit the market. Their arrival changed everything. Finally, people could visualize where they were right on the GPS receiver's screen. Now, digital mapping software—not receiver hardware—is the future of GPS, and the technology continues to evolve at a rapid rate. That means there's a lot of confusion among consumers about digital maps and software. Most of us have a hard time figuring out what separates one product from another. In this chapter we'll discuss:

• *What a digital map is and who collects the data*

• *What the difference is between a basemap, a proprietary map and third-party software*

• *Which digital maps are suitable for the kind of activity you enjoy most*

By the end of this chapter you'll know how to get the most out of your GPS receiver, its mapping software and all the different mapping software on the market designed to work with your GPS receiver. Furthermore, this chapter is designed to give you a solid foundation in understanding the basic concepts behind digital mapping. So even as digital mapping evolves, you won't be left out in the cold.

What is a Digital Map?

As you might remember from our discussion of paper maps in Chapter 4, there's nothing straightforward about any kind of map. There are map datums and coordinate systems to consider, among other things.

The only thing you need to know about digital maps is that they come in two different types: raster and vector. You won't see these terms used by software or GPS manufacturers, but it's important to understand the difference between them so you know what you can and can't do with your digital maps.

Raster map

A raster map is basically a digital picture of a paper map. If you took the "Redfield" USGS quad map that we used in Chapter 4 and put it on a computer scanner, the resulting digital image

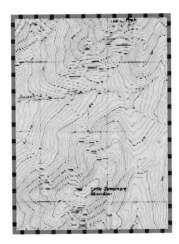

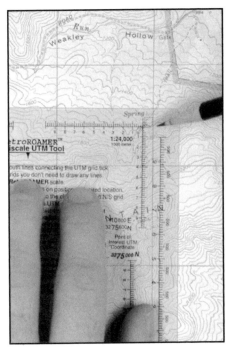

A raster map (above) is an electronic copy of a paper map (right). Each has advantages and disadvantages.

would be similar to a raster map. In fact, the illustrations used in Chapter 4 were taken from a raster map, not copies of a paper map. What's the advantage of a raster map then? Can't anyone take a picture of a map and have it blown up? That's not the same thing. A raster map is "georeferenced," which means that every square inch (cm) of the map and all the features on it—the highways, lakes, mountains and buildings—have specific GPS positions that can be expressed in the most popular coordinate systems, such as UTM and Lat/Lon.

The advantages that a raster map has over a paper map should be evident right off the bat. For one, all you have to do to get the GPS position of any point on the map is move the mouse cursor over that spot. If your GPS receiver has a basemap, then you've already seen how this works. Because a raster map is georeferenced, you can do lots of other things with it, such as measure distances between two points with the click of a button or get an elevation profile of a particular trail. We'll more fully discuss the advantages of raster maps later in the chapter.

The biggest disadvantage of raster maps is that they cannot be uploaded to your GPS receiver and can only be viewed on a computer screen. Raster maps take up a lot of memory, and GPS companies haven't done the work necessary to make their units read them. Only third-party software, such as National Geographic's Topo software, Maptech's Terrain Navigator or DeLorme's TopoUSA, among many others, use raster maps.

Vector map

Most people are already familiar with vector maps. These are the maps commonly found in car navigation systems. They are also found in proprietary mapping software sold by GPS manufacturers that work only with their units. If you're interested in loading electronic maps into your handheld GPS receiver, then you're looking for a vector product.

Vector maps have some great advantages. The software knows something specific about every single line on the map; and every line is tagged with information that you can't see. But your GPS receiver uses this hidden information to guide you around impassable objects (this is called "routing" or "turn-by-turn guidance") or display specific map details relevant to your activity.

For instance, a vector map can support extra layers of information about the locations of fishing holes not found on a raster map. Vector maps know that a side street is one-way. Raster maps are "dumb" by comparison. They don't know that a blue sec-

Routing and turn-by-turn guidance

Many people buy mapping software thinking that their handheld GPS receiver, uploaded with the appropriate maps, will tell them the best route to a given address. Expensive vehicle in-dash navigation systems can give you the shortest route from the airport to the hotel, and alert you when it's time to turn.

But be aware: Very few handheld GPS receivers or GPS mapping software packages are capable of giving you hands-free guidance to a location. The mapping software might display every little street and alley of a big city, and even list addresses to restaurants, but unless this software is specifically labeled "turn-by-turn" or "automatic routing," you'll have to plot your own route to a given address before you go.

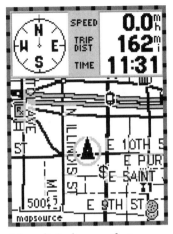

Most digital maps that are downloadable are optimized for vehicle navigation, not trailblazing.

tion of the map is in fact a lake, nor can they perform any routing functions.

Vector maps do have some disadvantages, however. They're mainly designed for vehicle navigation. Vector data hasn't been fully exploited yet for backcountry navigation. Perhaps the most important disadvantage to consider is that vector maps seldom contain all the information that would be found on any raster or USGS paper quad map.

Map makers

Who collects the data that ends up on a digital map—and why do you need to know? Virtually all the information you see on any map comes from government sources, such as NOAA, the USGS and so on. It doesn't matter whether it's a digital map or a paper map, a quad map, proprietary software sold by GPS manufacturers or third-party software.

So, since most maps come from the same sources, aren't they all the same? No. It's up to the software maker to pick and choose what ends up on their electronic maps, and that makes a huge difference in what you get.

The USGS 1:24,000-scale quad map is wonderfully detailed. Almost too detailed, according to some critics. How could a map be too detailed?

Consider the fact that it took the USGS about a hundred years to map the entire United States in 1:24,000 scale. They thought it would take ten years. Sure the maps are detailed, but all that detail on all those maps makes regular updating nearly impossible. That's not such a big deal with natural features, which don't change very much, if at all. But trails and man-made objects can change a lot from year to year. Some information on USGS quad maps is old or nonexistent. Cellular phone towers spring up like weeds, and new trail systems replace old.

Map updates might occur every ten years, and only then on the basis of popularity. National parks and areas that are used a lot get updated more often.

Basemaps

Collecting and compiling field data is an enormous task, much too big and expensive for individual companies to tackle on their own. If it took the U.S. government a hundred years to create a full set of 1:24,000-scale maps, just imagine how long it would take a GPS manufacturer to do the same! To make the basemaps that come preloaded in their receivers, GPS companies buy information from mapping companies that compile and organize field data collected by the U.S. government.

For the most part, a basemap is an interactive road atlas of major highways, roads and cities. Unless you live in the median of an interstate, you won't find your street on a basemap. Basemap information is updated fairly regularly. Unless it's specified for "marine" or some other special use, one GPS company's basemap is similar to the basemap found in any competitor's GPS receiver. A basemap is permanently fixed in a receiver's memory and cannot be modified or erased.

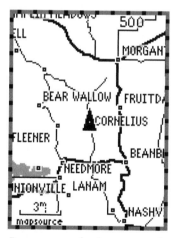

Basemaps only show general detail, like state roads and town locations.

All basemaps typically display the following: political boundaries or borders between states and countries; interstate highways, state roads, county routes and major city streets; locations of major cities and towns; major bodies of water and rivers.

Proprietary Maps

These are detailed electronic vector maps sold by GPS manu-
facturers to augment the more generalized basemaps in their
GPS receivers. Proprietary means that the company's maps
work only with their GPS receivers, no one else's. For example,
Magellan software won't work with a Garmin receiver; and
Garmin software won't work with a Magellan receiver.

Where does the information on proprietary maps come from?
GPS companies don't send their own people into the field to
collect the data for their proprietary maps. Too expensive.
Ironically, the data one GPS manufacturer uses to make its
maps usually comes from the same source that its competitor is
using to make its proprietary maps: the U.S. government. Or
the information comes from mapping companies that get their
data from public databases maintained by the government.

Proprietary maps are usually sold as a set of CD-ROMs, from
which you can upload information about selected areas into
your GPS receiver's memory. That means you have to hook up

your GPS receiver to a computer. For instance, if you're planning a road trip to Chicago, you might upload all of Chicago's city streets into your GPS receiver from a proprietary CD-ROM database. GPS receivers have a limited amount of memory, however, so you might need to upload new areas more than once during a long trip if you're traveling to different cities. And this means lugging along a laptop computer, cables and software.

There's a confusing array of proprietary mapping software out there aimed at boaters, anglers, tourists, hikers and hunters. How do you know what information is displayed on all these maps? First, always look for the map scale, which is usually listed on the box. At present, no GPS manufacturer makes large-scale maps similar in detail to a USGS 1:24,000 quad map. 1:100,000-scale maps are the most common.

Depending on their specific use, proprietary mapping software typically display one of the following groupings:

• For hikers and hunters. Forest land; rivers, lakes and streams; geysers and springs; mines; ridges and valleys; summits and peaks; swamps; visitor centers; camping and picnic areas; ranger stations; restaurants and lodges; select roads; main hiking trails.

• For boaters and anglers. Lakes, rivers and coastlines; buoys, lighthouses and other navigational aids; marinas; access roads; gas stations; some depth contours; known obstructions, such as shoals and sandbars.

• For tourists. City streets; cities and towns; airports; recreation and amusement parks; wineries; golf courses; tourist attractions; sport stadiums; museums; public gardens; campgrounds; zoos and aquariums.

As we now know, proprietary mapping software is based on vector data, and vector maps do not include all the information found on raster maps or paper quad maps. Something is always left out.

That's easy to see in mapping software made for marine use, for instance. In order to make room for memorizing depth contours and navigational aids, a particular GPS company may decide to leave out land features such as elevation contours and

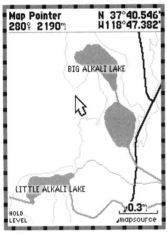

USGS quad map (top) showing location of hot spring to the west of Big Alkali Lake. Same area (bottom) on GPS screen displaying proprietary topo map software. Note difference in detail.

hiking trails. That's okay because you don't need that kind of information when you're on the water.

Still, you might be disappointed when you buy proprietary mapping software to suit a particular activity, only to discover that map features you wanted aren't on the digital maps you bought. Does that mean the data was never collected in the field? Not necessarily. The GPS company probably decided to leave it out in order to streamline their software so that it fit easily onto a CD-ROM, or so that data could be manipulated easier by the rather small amount of memory and slower processor speed of a GPS receiver.

Here's an example: Let's say you're going on a weekend hike. Before you leave, you upload regional maps from proprietary topographic software that has worked great on past hikes. On the trail you run into another hiker who tells you about a fantastic secluded hot spring a few miles away. He unfolds his paper map and shows you the location of the hot spring, but you don't bother getting the coordinates from his map into your GPS receiver. After all, your GPS receiver is already loaded with topo software of the area. And you want to get to the hot spring before dark. You part company with the friendly hiker and punch up the map page of your GPS receiver. But you can't find the hot spring anywhere. Why not? You saw it marked on the hiker's paper map; it should be on your map too, right?

Why isn't the hot spring on your digital map? Because the GPS company made an editing decision long before you bought their topo software. The GPS company isn't trying to cheat you. Only so much information can be squeezed onto a few CD-ROMs, and your GPS receiver can only display so much data. The vector data that the GPS company bought from the government to make their maps did indeed contain hot spring locations, but these locations were stripped out. The GPS company also stripped out every fifth contour line, and information about glaciers that they figured you wouldn't need.

And you never realized these map features were missing. Until today, when you really would've enjoyed a nice, relaxing soak in a secluded hot spring.

Third-Party Software

In addition to proprietary mapping software, many other software companies—called third-party companies because they're not directly associated with GPS manufacturers—make digital maps that work with your GPS receiver. At the moment, not a single GPS manufacturer allows third-party maps to be uploaded to their receivers. They're too busy promoting their own proprietary software. That means you cannot display third-party software on your GPS receiver.

You can, however, upload and display waypoints and routes that were created using third-party software, just not actual map features, such as elevation contours, trails, back roads and so on.

There are many excellent third-party software packages on the market targeted for a variety of uses, so it's only a matter of time before GPS companies make their receivers compatible with them. You may already be familiar with third-party mapping companies like National Geographic, DeLorme and MapTech. In fact, many of their products look very similar to the proprietary mapping software sold by GPS companies. Since you cannot display third-party maps on your GPS unit, what good is it? Why not just go with proprietary software?

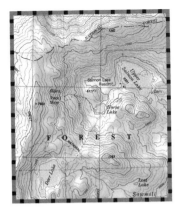

Well, third-party maps have a few distinct advantages over proprietary maps and paper maps. Since they come in both raster and vector formats, you often get the best of both technologies. Remember, proprietary maps consist of vector data only. The information on vector maps is limited to what the GPS manufacturer believes is relevant to your particular activity.

All of the big, third-party mapping companies sell software packages of 1:24,000-scale topographic maps in raster format, which are directly equivalent to the most detailed paper maps available anywhere, the USGS quad. These software packages can seem quite expensive, but compared to the cost of buying all the paper maps for a given region represented on a single CD-ROM, they're actually a very good deal. Especially considering that you can print your own customized paper maps every bit as good as a USGS paper quad.

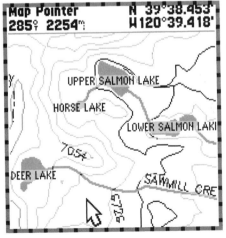

Top map detail was taken from a paper quad map. The middle map detail is from a third-party digital map of the same area. Note the density of detail equal to the quad map. The bottom map detail was taken from a proprietary digital "topo" map and displayed on a GPS receiver screen. Note the lack of detail.

More Detailed than USGS Quads?

Third-party mapping software can actually display more information than a USGS quad map. Wait, didn't I say earlier that the most detailed map available was a USGS paper quad? How can a digital map be more detailed than the source it's based on?

Let's return for a moment to our discussion of how maps are put together from a variety of public databases. The government doesn't have the resources to update every single USGS quad map every year, even though it might have new vector data sitting around in a database, waiting to be applied to a particular map. That's where third-party mapping companies come in. They can buy this new vector data set—for example, hiking trails in Adirondack State Park—and apply it to their products to create digital maps that will be actually more up-to-date than the current USGS quad maps for the same area. By extension, their maps are far more detailed than the proprietary topo maps sold by GPS companies.

If you've used USGS paper quad maps in the past, chances are you ran into the problem of having to carry two or three different maps to cover a particular area you want to visit. Unfortunately, the place you want to hike isn't always centered perfectly in the middle of the map. Sometimes you start out in the far corner of one map, then hike into an area represented by a second map, and end your trip on a third map.

Third-party digital raster maps can eliminate this inconvenience by seamlessly linking all the quad maps in a given region or state. So when you scroll past the natural edge of a map when planning your trip, you automatically move onto the adjoining map with no hiccups.

Which Type Is Best?

No matter what kind of digital mapping software you have, the best application for it is trip planning, before and after the trip. Proprietary mapping software shares many of the most powerful trip planning functions with third-party software, such as:

• *Creating waypoints and routes directly on the map and uploading them to your GPS unit*

- *Measuring distances between points*
- *Displaying elevation profiles of a particular trail or route*
- *Displaying 3-D views of a particular area*
- *Downloading waypoints and track logs directly to the map to see where you've been*

The advantage of using proprietary mapping software to plan your trip is being able to upload and download the entire map, waypoints and all, to and from your GPS receiver. With third-party software you can only upload or download waypoints, routes and track logs, but none of the actual map detail.

Considering that proprietary maps aren't as detailed as third-party maps, is this really an advantage for backcountry trip planning? No, it's not. The most important factor in trip planning is having the most detailed information possible.

To use our hot spring scenario from earlier in the chapter, we could have marked the location of that hot spring on our digital raster map and downloaded the coordinates to our GPS long before we hit the trail. That wasn't possible with the proprietary software, which didn't have any hot springs displayed anywhere on any of its maps because the GPS manufacturer stripped out all the vector data related to hot springs. But at least the proprietary map fit into your GPS receiver's memory!

Unless there's a big difference in specific map detail relevant to your trip—for example, 4x4 trails in Utah state parks—proprietary maps have the advantage over third-party maps when traveling by vehicle. Having map details and POI data available in real-time on your GPS receiver's display can't be beat, and you can even plan and edit your trip on the fly by marking waypoints and creating routes directly on the GPS receiver's map display. No computer required.

Conclusion

In an ideal world, we'd have detailed, seamless digital maps of the entire planet, instantly customizable for every possible activity, preloaded into our GPS receivers. We could tell the map what we wanted to do and where we wanted to do it, and the map would display relevant information about seasonal snowmobile trails in upstate New York, for instance, or city streets in London closed off due to construction, or successful summit approaches to a difficult Himalayan mountain peak.

Until that day, however, we'll have to make do with the hodge-podge of digital mapping products on the market. As long as you know what you're getting with your digital maps, and how to get the most out of them, you'll find that they're irreplaceable. You'll wonder how GPS receivers were ever sold without them.

CHAPTER 8

How to Buy a GPS Receiver

It couldn't be a better time to buy your first GPS receiver, or to upgrade your old one. Selective Availability, the government policy of degrading the accuracy of the GPS signal, has been discontinued for years now. 12-parallel-channel receivers are the norm, not the exception. Mapping units are common and reasonably priced, and digital mapping software continues to revolutionize how people use their GPS receivers in the field. GPS manufacturers are marketing a wide variety of GPS receivers to suit virtually every outdoor activity, and your GPS dollar gets you far more than it did a few years ago.

The only downside to all this technological advancement is figuring out which GPS receiver is the best one for you, now and in the future. This chapter will help you make that decision by focusing on three key areas that often separate one GPS receiver from another, including:

• *Hardware*

• *Software, screen size and controls*

• *Digital mapping*

The first question to ask yourself is "What do I want to do with my GPS receiver?" I already know the answer to this one: everything. You want a GPS receiver that works just as well in your truck as it does in the field and on your boat. You want one that has a big, color screen but is easy on batteries and weighs only 4 ounces (113 g). You want a unit that displays fully detailed topographic maps, sea charts and city streets, but doesn't need to be hooked up to a computer or require you to buy extra mapping software. It should give you pinpoint accuracy under all conditions. And it shouldn't cost more than a couple hundred bucks.

I can safely say that there is no such GPS receiver on the market, for any price. Buying a GPS receiver, like any sophisticated technology, means being objective about your needs, choices and budget. You can't have everything, and you really don't need everything. Before you set foot in the store, you should be absolutely clear about what you *most* want to do with your GPS receiver.

It's sort of like buying a car. If I bought what I thought I needed rather than being ruthlessly objective about it, there'd be a Corvette in my driveway instead of a Subaru. But then again, I can at least afford gas after buying the Subaru, and that makes it a hundred times more useful than the Corvette.

You say you're certain you need a GPS receiver for hiking and camping? That's not specific enough. Are you a day hiker or a wilderness survival nut? Do you consider sleeping in an RV to be camping? Or does camping mean digging your own snow cave and eating grubs and tree bark? You say you want a GPS receiver that will give you turn-by-turn guidance on a digital street map, for any city in the country. But 99% of the time you're driving back and forth to work. Sure it'd be neat to use a GPS receiver in the car on the way to work, but if you need it most for keeping track of your tree stands, then don't even consider receivers and software designed for automotive use.

Maybe you're not entirely sure what you might want to use a GPS receiver for, and that's fine, too. This chapter will help you sort through your priorities and narrow your choices.

Hardware

Hardware is the guts of your GPS receiver, the stuff you typically can't see. In the past, hardware separated good performance from bad, but nowadays, GPS hardware among competing manufacturers has reached a level of parity. The main areas to consider when selecting a GPS receiver are:

- *12-parallel-channel engine*
- *Antennas, including patch, quadrifilar/helix and external*
- *Accuracy, DGPS and WAAS*
- *Compasses, barometers, altimeters, etc.*

12-Parallel-Channel Engine

Less than ten years ago this was the most important category for choosing the right GPS receiver. And it wasn't much of a choice. Everyone wanted the new 12-parallel-channel units. There wasn't a very good argument other than price for hanging on to single- or dual-channel receivers. They didn't perform nearly as well in environments where GPS signals were blocked.

The good news is that receiver engines are no longer an issue. No matter what, buy a 12-parallel-channel receiver. In fact, you might not have a choice.

Antennas

No doubt you never gave a second thought to a GPS receiver's antenna, but you should. Keep in mind that in conditions where the GPS signal is blocked—under heavy tree canopy, in narrow canyons or "urban" canyons—no antenna can help you. The GPS satellite constellation is constantly shifting, and depending on what kind of antenna your GPS receiver has, certain satellites might be easier or harder to pick up at certain times.

There are three main types of antenna for handheld GPS receivers: patch, quadrifilar/helix-type and external.

Patch antennas. Most GPS receivers have patch antennas. You can't see a patch antenna because it's actually inside the case, under the flat piece of plastic above the display.

Because it's natural to hold a GPS receiver like a television remote control, patch antennas are always facing upward at the sky when you're operating your GPS unit. That makes patch antennas very good at picking up satellites directly overhead, and not quite as good at picking up satellite signals that are skimming in over the horizon on a flatter angle.

Most hikers and hunters use their GPS receivers periodically, not continuously, so this isn't really an issue. For driving, however, a patch antenna will have a harder time keeping a lock on signals in less-than-perfect conditions, because most overhead satellite signals are blocked by the vehicle's cabin. You might lose navigation information at a critical moment.

In a nutshell, patch antennas are:

• *Good at picking up signals overhead, but not as good at picking up signals lower on the horizon*

• *Better suited for use in the field and on the water than in a vehicle*

• *More streamlined than quadrifilar antennas*

Quadrifilar or helix type antennas. Unlike patch antennas, quadrifilar and helix antennas actually look like antennas. GPS receivers with these antennas are somewhat bulkier than receivers with patch antennas because of the separate plastic "stick" attached to the case. Inside that stick is a wire coil that picks up satellite signals, and it can be rotated or swiveled to better receive signals low on the horizon.

Theoretically, helix antennas aren't quite as good as patch antennas at picking up satellites directly overhead, but I've never had such a problem, even with the antenna oriented toward the ground. The big advantage of a helix antenna is that you can hold and operate a GPS receiver in almost any position because the antenna can be adjusted so that it always faces the sky. That makes it easier to mount the GPS unit on the dashboard of a vehicle, or on the handlebars of an ATV.

Quadrifilar or helix antennas are:

• *Good at picking up signals lower on the horizon, and better in general at picking up satellite signals from any direction*

• *Well suited for use in any environment, especially in vehicles*

• *Bulkier than patch antennas*

External antennas. If you're serious about using your handheld GPS receiver in a vehicle, you'll be disappointed by its performance. Consider buying an external antenna. It looks like a miniature computer mouse, with a long cord attached to it that allows you to place the antenna on the car roof, or wedged between the windshield and dashboard. Then you can mount your GPS receiver closer to where you can actually see it—that is, if your receiver isn't specially designed for use in vehicles.

I've also seen hikers with external antennas attached to their hats, with their GPS receivers stowed away in a cargo pocket or backpack. This might be a little extreme, but it works very well.

If you're undecided about external antennas but want to keep your options open, make sure the GPS receiver you buy comes with an external antenna jack.

External antennas:

• *Are the best choice for use in vehicles*

• *Require an external antenna jack on your GPS receiver*

• *Can be used in the field, but only by techno hiker geeks*

Accuracy, DGPS and WAAS

Accuracy is not an issue when comparing different models and brands of GPS receivers. All are capable of 49-foot (15-m) accuracy. You can increase accuracy in one of two ways: attach DGPS hardware to your GPS receiver or use a WAAS-enabled receiver, which is actually a software modification.

Unless you're using your GPS receiver exclusively on major waterways, forget about DGPS. It's not meant for land use. WAAS-enabled receivers don't require any additional hardware and they work great anywhere, although they cost a bit more and WAAS signals aren't as effective at higher latitudes. Considering what you get—10- to 16-foot (3- to 5-m) accuracy—WAAS-enabled receivers are well worth the added cost. If your GPS budget is tight, think of other areas where you can cut costs in order to afford a WAAS-enabled unit.

Compass, Barometer, Altimeter

For the added cost, it really isn't worth buying a GPS receiver with a built-in compass, barometer or altimeter. It's the kind of thing that sounds nifty but in all practical reality you'll use the added features about as often as you eat your camp dinners with a big, fat Swiss Army knife that has a fork and spoon in it. Likewise, would you buy a car that had a built-in bicycle? Probably not.

If you're serious about backcountry navigation and orienteering, the compass built into a GPS receiver is useless. The same goes for the built-in barometer/altimeter designed to give more precise altitude measurements. If you're that keen to get precise altitude information, you want a separate altimeter; otherwise, plot your waypoints on a digital or paper map and use the elevation data.

Software, Screen Size and Controls

You'll be surprised how subtle differences in software among GPS manufacturers, and even among models from the same manufacturer, make all the difference in how you use your GPS receiver. I learned how to use GPS on units that are now fifteen years old, and I consider newer units difficult to use. Of course, newer units are much easier to use for just about anybody except me. That should tell you something. The user-friendliness of software, controls and displays is very subjective. The important thing is that you're comfortable using your GPS receiver, so when it's time to buy, pay particular attention to:

• Waypoints, routes and track logs

• Screen size/display resolution, including backlighting and color displays

• Keypads and soft keys, including user interface

• Size

Waypoints, Routes and Track Logs

Even bare-bones GPS receivers have more than enough storage capacity for waypoints (500), routes (up to 20) and track log points (2,000). But, please don't base any part of your decision on this category alone.

If you think you're going to need an extraordinary amount of waypoint and route capacity, there are other ways to achieve your goals. For instance, the most basic, inexpensive GPS software on the market—not necessarily expensive mapping software—allows you to download waypoints, routes and track logs into a computer database for safekeeping.

Most GPS receivers allow you to reverse a track log or turn it into a route that automatically guides you back to your original starting point. GPS companies have different names for this very useful feature, usually some variation on "backtrack" or "track back," and so on. If you're not sure if a GPS receiver has this feature, ask the salesperson or call the manufacturer.

Screen Size/Display Resolution

Depending upon your activity, the screen size and display resolution of a GPS receiver will decide whether you actually use it. You will have to compromise. Most of us want a small, lightweight unit that's easy on batteries, but we want a big screen that's easy to see under any conditions. These are competing demands. Remember the rule: Be realistic about what you want to do with your GPS receiver.

If you know you'll be using digital maps a lot, in the field or in a car, get the biggest screen possible, even if it means sacrificing smaller size, lighter weight and longer battery life. Nothing is more frustrating than scrolling around a tiny map display that's already made smaller by data fields, trying to locate a POI, land feature or waypoint. What's the point of spending all that money on digital maps and larger memory capacity if you can't see the map adequately?

If you'll be using maps periodically or only as a reference, go with the smaller screen and do your trip planning on the computer.

For drivers, size, weight and battery life are of little concern, so get the biggest screen you can afford.

Display resolution is another important factor. A small GPS receiver with a high-resolution display will be easier to read than a receiver with a larger, lower resolution screen. That's because more pixels make what's on the screen, such as map features, numbers, text and graphics, sharper and clearer.

If you want to use digital maps a lot in the field—not necessarily at home, where you'll be using a computer—get the highest resolution display you can afford. Pixel ratios range widely, from a crude 64 x 128 to a fine 160 x 288, and even higher for GPS receivers designed for use in vehicles.

All GPS receivers have backlighting that allows you to see the display in low light. Backlighting, however, chews up battery life very quickly. Check to see how easy it is to turn on the backlighting. With some GPS receivers it might be too easy to accidentally toggle the backlighting button and drain the batteries (I've done it many times).

Color displays are becoming more and more popular, and in the store they look great, especially with a digital map loaded. Rivers and lakes are blue, roads and highways are red or black, forests are green. In the field color screens are just a novelty, and they use up precious battery life twice as fast as traditional 4-level gray-scale displays. Plus, they cost a lot more. My advice? Don't waste your money unless you're using your GPS receiver exclusively inside a vehicle, with a 12-volt cigarette lighter adapter as a power source.

In the past, some GPS receivers had the odd characteristic of appearing blank when viewed while wearing polarized sunglasses. Manufacturers rectified the problem, but the example highlights a good point. Anglers, boaters and oftentimes drivers wear dark, polarized sunglasses to reduce glare. If you have a difficult time reading the display of a GPS receiver on land, for whatever reason (maybe you're farsighted), it's not going to be any easier reading the display on the water while you're wearing dark sunglasses and bouncing over waves. You can adjust the contrast of the LCD display in the receiver's setup menu, but that might not be good enough. You might want to consider buying a fixed-mount GPS receiver with a big display designed specifically for use on boats.

Keypads and Soft Keys

Don't ignore ergonomics when shopping for a GPS receiver. If you can't comfortably operate the GPS receiver then you can forget about any of its other qualities. Handheld GPS receivers can't be easily operated while wearing gloves, for instance, because the buttons are too small and placed too close together. Bigger buttons with more space between them can be operated more easily when bouncing over waves or rough roads, but that might mean buying a unit bigger than you want. What about pushing buttons when your bare fingers are freezing cold? Are the keys clearly labeled? Remember what you want to do most with your GPS receiver and try to imagine the conditions when you'll be using it most. While walking? Sitting? At night?

Most GPS receivers have controls on their face, below the display. To reduce size, some manufacturers put soft keys (covered in rubber) on the sides of the unit as well. This means you can't see the buttons in order to manipulate information on the screen. Are you comfortable with this layout? Are you coordinated enough to use it with one hand? What if it's mounted on a dashboard of a vehicle—can you reach the buttons without taking your eyes off the road, possibly swerving or, worse, crashing?

The rocker keypad (the big button with the four directional arrows on it) will be used most often. Is it comfortable? Can you reach it with the thumb of the hand holding the receiver? My GPS receivers have always had rocker keypads, so I have a tough time getting used to some of the newer "stick" type keys on smaller units. I hate having to use two hands to operate units with this sort of layout. But that's a personal preference. Don't be shy about evaluating a GPS receiver based on how easy it is to operate.

When you don't know much about GPS, it's difficult to evaluate the user interface. By "user interface" I mean what you see when you press the buttons, and how easy or difficult it is to manipulate information on the screen. User interfaces vary widely between models and brands. Some are friendly, some are like trying to program your VCR with a manual written in another language.

Take the time to scroll through the main page sequence: satellite status, position, compass/highway, map/plotter. Does it make sense? You'll probably be spending most of your time on the map and compass pages, so pay close attention to them. Are they easy to get to? Can you easily change the information on them? How many keystrokes does it take to, say, reorient the map? More than you'd like? Are there dedicated zoom keys to change the map scale (better)? Or do you have to change the scale through the menu options (annoying)?

Once you've evaluated the main-page sequence, try to punch up the main menu. If you'll be working with digital or paper maps, you'll spend a lot of time in your receiver's menu system changing coordinate systems, map datums, map features, navigation information and so on. How many keystrokes does it take to accomplish any of these tasks?

How about searching for waypoints and routes in the unit's database? I find that I'm always using one or two older GPS receivers that have dedicated "Menu" keys that allow me to get to information quicker. I have newer units with more and better features, but they don't have a dedicated Menu key, and I end up wandering around submenus looking for what I want. I'd much rather use an older GPS receiver with fewer features that allows me to get the information I want, fast.

Again, that's a personal preference, not a rule. Sometimes, old dogs *can't* learn new tricks. The point is to know your personal preferences. If the user-interface doesn't "feel" right now, it probably won't feel any better later. Go with your gut.

Size and Weight

People who spend a lot of time in the backcountry are usually weight freaks. They can guess the weight of any item in their backpacks to the nearest ounce or gram. To say size doesn't matter is heresy to these people. It's not wise, however, to buy a GPS receiver based upon size and weight alone.

Smaller and lighter might be better if you're talking about camp stoves or sleeping bags, but not when it comes to GPS. The difference between a fully featured GPS receiver and the smallest, no frills receiver—not counting the combination wristwatch/GPS receivers, which are virtually useless—is no more than 4 or 5 ounces (113 or 142 g). Cost aside, what are you getting for that extra weight? On one hand, a waterproof GPS receiver with a decent-sized screen and digital mapping capabilities. On the other hand, an extra pair of socks. Which 4 ounces has more value?

Digital Mapping

The hottest GPS receivers on the market right now are digital mapping units, and they're also among the most expensive. This category is where you can blow your whole GPS budget, so be extra careful.

As we've learned, GPS receivers come in a dizzying array of flavors, some with basemaps, some without, some with a small amount of programmable flash memory, some with a lot of memory. Then there's the mapping software itself, which is even more confusing. What software works with what GPS receivers? What software is best for the day hiker versus the serious hiker? A weekend angler versus an offshore cruiser? The daily driver versus the traveling salesman?

Before we get too far into this topic, I'm going to make a few simple recommendations that might surprise you. They are:

• Spend the money on a GPS receiver with a good basemap. Forget plain-vanilla GPS receivers without basemaps.

• For serious hiking, hunting or other backcountry activity, don't waste your money on buying a GPS receiver with downloadable mapping capabilities.

• Consider a mapping unit if you are using a GPS receiver in a car or boat, or if you simply enjoy having the latest and greatest toy.

Basemaps

GPS receivers with built-in basemaps have been around for a long time, so you won't be paying for the development costs of a new technology and you still get all the advantages.

While limited, basemaps are great tools. A typical basemap will show interstates and state highways, major metropolitan thoroughfares, cities, airports, lakes, rivers and exit information for places such as restaurants, hotels and gas stations.

Basemaps are great for drivers going from Point A to Point B and needing to know distances to major land features. Even when I'm 20 miles (32 km) from the nearest road, I use my GPS receiver's basemap to orient myself.

What's on the Map?

That's the most important question you need to answer before buying any GPS receiver with mapping capabilities, or GPS mapping software. Don't ask what you can do with an electronic map. That's fairly obvious: You can see yourself in relationship to land features. What you really need to know is if the land features you need most are pictured on the map. The sidestreets, the navigation buoys, the contours, the hiking trails—are they actually on the map? If not, forget it.

The current state of digital mapping is being driven by vehicle navigation (no pun intended). For the GPS manufacturer, that's where the money is. There are more people who own cars than there are people who hike, hunt and birdwatch added together. Digital maps, whether they're third-party software or proprietary maps that you upload into your GPS receiver, are great for motorized travel of any kind. The fact is, proprietary topographic software is not as detailed as a thirty-year-old paper map, or third-party raster maps.

So why spend extra money on an inferior technology? So that you can display that inferior technology on your GPS receiver in the field? Is that really more of an advantage than, say, taking a USGS quad map into the field? Or planning your trip using third-party software and uploading waypoints, instead of inferior maps, into your GPS receiver? The answer to both questions is no.

For marine navigation, it makes sense to have a GPS receiver to which you can upload proprietary marine software. The sorts of map features you need to know about most—boat ramps, shoals, obstructions—aren't mere conveniences. Knowing exactly where you are in relation to marine features, even some of them, may save your life, or at least your propeller.

Memory

Assuming you have your heart set on a GPS receiver with mapping capabilities, your next decision will be about how much memory you should spring for. That's an easy one: as much as you can afford. Why? The law of technology says that memory requirements increase exponentially with every new product release. My first computer had 20 megabytes of hard drive space! That's not enough to store even a few high-resolution digital photos. As maps and databases become more sophisticated and complex, which they most certainly will, your memory capacity requirements will skyrocket.

The first GPS receivers with the ability to upload street maps had less than 2 megabytes of programmable flash memory. Today, you can get GPS receivers with 128 megabytes of memory. That's the one you want. 16 or 32 megabytes might seem like enough for most uses, and you'll get by on that much memory for a while. But your GPS receiver will be outdated sooner by increasing memory demands.

Appendix

GPS Terms and Definitions

2D Operating Mode

A two-dimensional GPS position fix that includes only latitude and longitude, not elevation. Your receiver must be locked onto a minimum of three satellites for a 2D fix and the satellite status page will indicate this. Because your GPS isn't using as many satellite signals to calculate a 2D position, it's less accurate than navigating in 3D mode.

3D Operating Mode

A three-dimensional GPS position fix that includes horizontal coordinates and elevation. You need to be locked onto at least four satellites. Most of the time your GPS will operate in 3D mode, as long as you have a relatively clear view of the sky. Now and then as you pass under dense tree cover or navigate in tight places where the sky is partially blocked from view, your GPS receiver will drop into 2D mode and will indicate as such on the satellite status page.

A

Accuracy

GPS receivers are capable of getting you within 49 feet (15 m)—at worst—of a known location, such as a waypoint. Oftentimes it will give you much greater accuracy. If your GPS receiver is WAAS-enabled, accuracy narrows to a maximum of 15 feet (4.5 m), at least in the United States. All else being equal, such as number of channels, accuracy is not an issue between different brands and models of GPS receivers. One brand is as accurate as the next, no matter what the manufacturer or the salesperson says.

Acquisition Time

Every time you turn on your GPS receiver it needs to collect information from satellites to figure out where it is. Depending upon the last time you used it, or whether you've traveled over 300 miles (483 km) from the last place in which you used it, acquisition time can be a matter of seconds or minutes. See also Cold Start and Initialization.

Active Antenna

An active antenna amplifies the GPS signal before sending it to the receiver for processing and is generally better at picking up weak signals.

Active Leg

When navigating a specified route, this is the segment that you're on at any given moment. A segment is a part of a route between any two waypoints. If your route is made up of points A, B, C, D and E, and you're almost to the end, your active leg is probably D to E. Other legs you used to get there are A to B, B to C and C to D.

Alarm

This is your GPS receiver's way of letting you know how close you are to a designated location. You set the distance from the location for the alarm to go off. That way you can keep your eyes on the trail, road or marker buoys instead of your GPS receiver. Alarms can be turned off, such as for hunting applications.

Almanac/Almanac Data

Every satellite in the GPS constellation transmits a detailed calendar about where it's going to be at any one time, in addition to orbit and health information about all the other satellites. When your GPS receiver is in acquisition mode, it's reviewing this information so it knows where to look for satellites that might not be in view at the moment.

Altimeter

An instrument that measures altitude or elevation with respect to a reference point, usually sea level, by means of air pressure. Some GPS receivers come with built-in altimeters that work independently of the elevation reading calculated from GPS signals, which can be less accurate.

Atomic Clock

At the heart of every GPS satellite are very precise clocks that keep time based on the predictable movement of cesium or rubidium atoms. A cesium clock has an error rate of one second per million years. Your GPS receiver, however, keeps time in a more conventional and less accurate manner, which is one reason you won't ever get 100% accuracy with it.

Availability

The number of hours per day that a particular location has enough satellites in view to enable a GPS position fix. The floor of a box canyon has low availability. An intersection in the middle of the desert has high availability. When the full constellation of GPS satellites had yet to be launched, early GPS users could only use their receivers for short periods of time and only in specific places.

Azimuth

Another word for bearing. Specifically, it's the angle of measurement between the horizon and a satellite, or some other object, measured clockwise in degrees from a north or south reference line. It can be referenced to true north, grid north or magnetic north. The reverse direction is called a back azimuth or back bearing.

Azimuth Ring

The dial on a compass, marked from zero to 360 degrees.

B

Backlight

Illuminates both the display and keypad so you can operate your GPS receiver at night. It's a good idea to switch the backlight off as a matter of course until you really need it. Otherwise, bring extra batteries.

Basemap

Many GPS receivers come off the shelf with permanent, built-in maps, or basemaps, that typically include features unlikely to change much: rivers and lakes, cities and towns, highways and state roads, airports, state borders and so on. Basemaps make it very convenient to navigate to most places that you might find on a road map, but you'll need to supplement the basemap with additional, downloadable maps for more specific uses, such as topographic maps for hikers and hunters, or sea charts for anglers.

Beacon

A stationary transmitter that emits signals in all directions. An example is differential GPS (DGPS). Used almost exclusively by boaters, DGPS correction signals are sent from a beacon transmitter and require a separate "beacon" receiver to pick them up and send them to a regular GPS receiver for processing.

Bearing

The compass direction between one point and another or, practically speaking, the direction you want to be going toward a specific destination or waypoint, measured to the nearest degree. Your bearing is not your course or track, because it rarely involves traveling in a straight line.

Benchmark

A permanent object, natural or man-made, with a known elevation. A benchmark can be used as a reference point when navigating a route or in determining the elevation of nearby land features.

Breadcrumb Trail

Also called a track log. Your GPS receiver automatically stores track-log points or breadcrumbs of your path from the moment you turn it on. The distance between the breadcrumbs can be adjusted to suit certain kinds of travel, or the entire trail can be made into a route. The breadcrumb trail shows up on your receiver's map page as a dotted line behind your direction of movement.

C

Carrier

The frequency of an unmodulated output of a radio transmitter. The GPS L1 carrier frequency is 1575.42 MHz. Your GPS receiver is tuned to this carrier frequency.

Cartography

The science and art of making maps, including construction of projections, design, compilation of data, drafting and reproduction. Many GPS receivers have detailed mapping—or cartographic—capabilities. That doesn't mean they can make maps, but they can display maps and manipulate them electronically.

Channel

A channel of a GPS receiver consists of the circuitry necessary to receive the signal from a single GPS satellite. Most GPS receivers have many channels dedicated to receiving satellite signals to increase the speed and accuracy of their calculations.

Cliff

A high, steep rock face. On a topographic map, a cliff is portrayed by contour lines running close together or sometimes merging into a single line. The closer the lines, the more sheer the cliff.

Clock Bias

The difference between the time indicated by the clock in your GPS receiver and the time given by the atomic clock in the GPS satellite (also called true universal time).

Clock Offset

A constant difference in the time reading between two clocks, usually due to the fact that the clocks are in different time zones. You can set the clock offset in your GPS to account for this difference.

Cold Start

Turning on a GPS receiver after it has been turned off for a long time, is new out of the box, or has traveled more than 300 miles (483 km) since the last time it was used. If you don't help the receiver figure out roughly where it is by "initializing" it, it will search for satellites by itself, a procedure that may take several minutes before a position fix is achieved.

Compass Rose

A circle or similar design that includes graduated degrees and looks like the face of a compass, printed on a chart or map for reference. Your GPS receiver has an electronic compass rose to make it easier to see your bearing, track and other position information relative to compass direction.

Constellation

A set of GPS satellites is often referred to as a constellation, like a group of stars, although GPS satellites are not fixed in the sky. The GPS constellation is constantly shifting overhead as satellites come in and out of range of your GPS receiver.

Contour Interval

The difference in elevation, in feet or meters, between two adjacent contour lines, as indicated in the map legend.

Contour Line

A line on a map that connects points of equal elevation. On areas of the map that are relatively flat, there may be light or broken supplementary contour lines to indicate the shape of land that might not be perceivable because the distance between regular contour lines is too large. A depression contour line indicates an area of lower elevation than surrounding terrain and has small hachures pointing inward.

Control Point

Also called a control station, or monument, to which precise coordinates have been assigned. The National Geodetic Survey maintains a nationwide network of control points that are used almost exclusively by land surveyors and other high-end users as reference points.

Control Segment

One of the three GPS segments. This portion refers to the ground-based network of monitoring stations that manage the accuracy of GPS satellite orbits and clocks. There's also the user segment (you) and the space segment (the satellites).

Coordinate

A set of numbers that describes your exact location on earth. Coordinates are typically based on latitude/longitude lines of reference, or a global/regional grid projection, such as UTM, LAT/LON, etc.

Course

Direction from the beginning landmark of a route to its destination, or the direction from one waypoint on a route to the next waypoint.

Course/Acquisition (C/A) Code

The standard GPS code used by civilian GPS receivers. It contains the information the GPS receiver needs to fix its position and time, and is accurate to 49 feet (15 m) or better, but is less precise than military GPS receivers, which use P-code.

Course Deviation Indicator (CDI)

Displays how far off course you are in going from one point to another.

Course Made Good (CMG)

The bearing from your starting point to your present position, or the ground you covered up to your present position as you meander toward your destination.

Course Over Ground (COG)

Your direction of movement relative to a position on the ground.

Course To Steer

The heading you need to maintain in order to reach a destination.

Course-Up Orientation

Setting the map page of your GPS receiver so that your direction of travel, or course, is always facing "up" on the display.

Crosstrack Error (XTE/XTK)

The distance you are off an intended course in either direction.

D

Datum

Since the earth is round and maps need to be flat to fit in our pockets, people have been devising methods to flatten the earth, at least theoretically, for centuries. These theories are called datums, which are mathematical models of the earth as if it were flat. Different countries at different periods in history used different datums to create their maps. Maps that are created using different datums will show the same latitude/longitude, but in slightly different locations. "Slightly" can be dangerous. When using a GPS receiver with a map or chart, it's very important that the datums match up, otherwise you could run aground on a reef, take the wrong trail or drive off a cliff. Your GPS receiver defaults to the popular WGS-84 datum, which is fine for most applications. But many topographic maps carried by hikers and hunters use the NAD-27 or NAD-83 datum. To say nothing of sea charts, which can vary widely. Always check the legend on your map or chart and adjust your GPS receiver's datum accordingly before you set out on any adventure.

Dead Reckoning

The process of determining your present position by projecting course and speed from a past known position. Or, predicting a future position by projecting course and speed from a known present position. For instance, if you're going 5 mph (8 kmph) at a heading of 58 degrees, you can draw a line on the map from your present position to figure out where you might be an hour from now. Dead reckoning results in only an approximate position.

Depression

A natural or man-made hole in the terrain that may contain water. See also Contour Line.

Differential GPS (DGPS)

This applies almost exclusively to offshore boaters and anglers since DGPS beacons are found only on the coasts, in addition to shorelines of major bodies of water, such as the Great Lakes and the Mississippi

River. DGPS beacons know exactly where they are, so they can check their known location against the GPS signal and calculate how far off it is (the "differential"). After adjusting the error, it broadcasts a correction message to GPS receivers in the area capable of receiving it. Not all GPS receivers can accept a DGPS signal. It requires a special antenna and software. But the increase in accuracy is significant—better than 3 feet (1 m)—which is ideal for commercial vessel traffic trying to navigate tricky ports, or anglers trying to find that secret hole where the big fish hang out. The U.S. Coast Guard maintains the DGPS system.

Dilution of Precision (DOP)

A term describing how satellite geometry affects accuracy, expressed as a DOP value (not an issue for boaters and anglers, where there's almost always a wide open sky overhead). Positions tagged with a higher DOP value are less accurate than those tagged with a lower DOP.

Dithering

By introducing "noise" to the GPS signal, at one time the DoD made civilian GPS receivers less accurate than they could've been. This practice was called Selective Availability. But the DoD has since stopped the practice.

DoD

The United States Department of Defense. The DoD manages the Global Positioning System.

Drainage

The entire area drained by a river and all its tributaries; a small valley.

Draw

A small, natural depression; a gully; the upper part of a small stream valley.

E

Elevation

The distance above or below average sea level. For reasons geometric in nature, GPS receivers don't calculate elevation or vertical measurements as accurately as they do horizontal measurements. Generally, elevation readings are 50% less accurate than your EPE. If your EPE is 10 meters (33 feet), then elevation can be off by as much as 15 meters (49 feet).

Ellipsoid

A geometric surface, all of whose plane sections are either ellipses or circles. Datums are based on ellipsoid models of the earth.

Ephemeris Data

Current satellite position and timing information transmitted as part of the satellite data message. A set of ephemeris data is valid for several hours. Errors originating in the ephemeris data can decrease the accuracy of your GPS receiver, but they can be corrected with DGPS and WAAS.

Estimated Position Error (EPE)

An estimation of your position accuracy at any given moment based on the geometry and position of tracked satellites, time clock offset, satellite signal quality and so on. Your EPE is often shown on the satellite status page.

Estimated Time Enroute (ETE)

The time it will take to reach your destination based upon your present position, speed and course.

Estimated Time of Arrival (ETA)

The estimated time you will arrive at a destination.

F

Federal Radionavigation Plan (FRP)

It lays out plans and budget for the entire GPS system, forecasts usage by various parties, such as boaters or commercial transportation, and names which agency is going to manage which part of the system. You can find the FRP online at the Department of Transportation website.

G

Geocaching

A game that resembles large-scale hide-and-seek. Teams of geocachers use GPS receivers and a set of coordinates to find hidden items that may be many miles apart.

Geographic Information System (GIS)

A computer system or software capable of assembling, storing, manipulating and displaying geographically referenced information (i.e., data identified according to their location). In practical use, GIS often refers to the computer system, software, data collection equipment, personnel and actual data. GIS software is used to create the electronic maps that are either built into or downloadable to your GPS receiver. When you move your GPS receiver's map cursor over a road or some other feature, you have GIS to thank for the instant latitude and longitude reading that pops up.

Geometric Dilution of Precision (GDOP)

See Dilution of Precision (DOP).

Geosynchronous Orbit

A satellite that orbits the earth at the same speed of the earth's rotation, so that it stays over one spot all the time. The two WAAS satellites are in geosynchronous orbit. Regular GPS satellites are not.

Global Orbiting Navigation Satellite System (GLONASS)

The Russian version of our GPS.

Global Positioning System (GPS)

A constellation of 24 satellites orbiting the earth at an altitude of 12,000 miles (19,000 km) and providing very precise, worldwide positioning and navigation information 24 hours per day, seven days per week, in any weather and to anyone in the world with a GPS receiver. A GPS receiver pinpoints its position on earth by measuring its distance from the GPS satellites, calculating the time it takes for a coded radio signal to reach it.

GoTo

A convenient function of most GPS receivers is the capability to "go to" any location you choose simply by pressing a dedicated key marked GOTO or selecting GoTo from a menu. Once GoTo is activated, your GPS receiver will guide you to the destination until you either reach it or cancel it. Another way to look at the GoTo function is as a one-legged route, with your present position at one end and your selected destination at the other end.

Grid

Also called coordinate system, a grid is a pattern of regularly spaced horizontal and vertical lines that form square zones on a map, with some kind of reference used to establish points. A grid example is the UTM system.

H

Hachure

Short lines or "hash marks" used to represent relief features on a map and often run perpendicular to contour lines. Each hachure line lies in the direction of the steepest slope. Lines that are closer together or thicker denote steeper slopes, and lines that are farther apart or thinner denote gentler slopes.

Heading

The direction in which a vehicle is moving. For air and sea operations, your heading may differ from actual Course Over Ground (COG) due to winds or currents forcing you off course.

Healthy

A GPS satellite that stays in its orbit, keeps its clock clean and transmits good, accurate signals. Your GPS receiver knows the health of all the satellites in the GPS constellation, and it ignores the signals of those with poor health.

I

Icon

A graphic symbol attached to a waypoint, such as a fish or skull and crossbones, that shows up on the map or plotter page of your GPS receiver. You're not required to assign every waypoint an icon to remember it by. But it's much easier to see where you are in relation to things when waypoints are tagged with icons rather than little snippets of text that may look the same.

Initialization

When you first take your GPS receiver out of the box, or when you turn it on after traveling a long distance, it's feeling a little lost. To help orient your GPS receiver so that it locks onto satellites quicker, you have to give it a rough idea of where it is on the planet. Usually this requires little more than choosing a continent and then a specific region or state, from a menu. After initialization, the receiver remembers its last location and acquires a position more quickly the next time it's turned on because it knows where to look for satellites (by storing almanac data in its memory). See also Cold Start and Acquisition Time.

Input/Output (I/O)

The two-way transfer of GPS information with another device, such as an autopilot or another GPS unit.

Invert/Reverse Route

If you reach the end of a route and want to return to the beginning, most GPS receivers allow you to flip-flop the route by inverting or reversing it through the menu. This is not the same as using the "backtrack" feature that automatically turns a track log into a route.

Ionosphere

The electrically charged region of the earth's atmosphere that warps and ripples around the earth as it's buffeted by solar winds. GPS satellite signals, which are merely low-frequency radio waves, are affected by the ever-changing thickness of the ionosphere, a largely unpredictable source of error that will prevent civilian GPS receivers from ever achieving 100% accuracy.

L

L1 Frequency

One of two radio frequencies transmitted by GPS satellites (1575.42 MHz), L1 carries both the civilian C/A code and the military P-code.

L2 Frequency

The other radio frequency (1227.6 MHz) transmitted by GPS satellites, carrying only the P-code used by the military. Your GPS receiver is blind to this signal.

Latitude

The distance of a point on the earth's surface north or south of the equator, perpendicular to the earth's polar axis, and measured by degrees from zero to 90. This distance is measured in degrees, minutes and seconds. One minute of latitude equals one nautical mile (1.85 km). For the spatially challenged, think of latitude as a series of horizontal rings wrapping around the earth parallel to the equator.

Leg

A portion of a route consisting of a starting waypoint and a destination waypoint. A route that is comprised of waypoints A, B, C and D would contain three legs. The route legs would be from A to B, from B to C and from C to D.

Line-Of -Sight (LOS) Propagation

The Achilles heel of GPS receivers is their dependence on line-of-sight radio wave propagation, which is another way of saying if something gets between you and your GPS unit, you might lose the satellite signals entirely. If you've ever driven under a bridge or through a tunnel in the middle of your favorite song on the radio, you understand the concept. The sound crackles or disappears altogether into static. Thick, leafy tree canopy, tall buildings or canyon walls, even the cabin of a boat or roof of your car will block GPS satellite signals. Powerful multi-channel receiver designs have mitigated this problem, but nothing short of ridiculously tall antennas will solve it.

Lithium

A soft, silvery, highly reactive metallic element that is used in batteries where weight and cold weather conditions are concerns.

Local Area Augmentation System (LAAS)

For pilots only, LAAS beacons are ground-based DGPS installed around airports to support precision aircraft landings in a local area (20-mile/32-km range). Your GPS receiver can't take advantage of the improved accuracy given by LAAS.

Longitude

The distance east or west of the Prime Meridian, measured in degrees, minutes and seconds, of a point on the earth's surface. Lines (meridians) of longitude create a geographic grid around the world and are not parallel, but rather converge at the poles. For the spatially challenged, think of each meridian as beginning at the North Pole and running vertically to the South Pole (as the earth is commonly depicted, with North America at the top and the tip of South America pointing to the bottom).

LORAN

Stands for LOng RAnge Navigation. One of the first radio navigation technologies, coastal LORAN stations transmit a grid of radio waves that allows for accurate position plotting. Special shipboard LORAN receivers interpret these signals and provide readings that correspond to a grid overprinted on nautical charts. By comparing signals from two different stations, much in the way your GPS receiver compares signals from satellites, the mariner can determine his or her position. LORAN will eventually be phased out.

M

Magnetic Declination

The difference, in degrees, between true north and magnetic north. A topographic map is always oriented to true north, but a compass always points toward magnetic north. In actuality, the two are 1,300 miles (2,093 km) apart. An imaginary line passes through both magnetic and true north (currently it travels in a southeasterly direction through the U.S. from near the Great Lakes to the Deep South). Along this line it is not necessary to adjust a compass for magnetic declination. But west and east of the line you have to adjust the degree of deviation for that particular geographic area, as indicated on the map. Your GPS receiver doesn't rely on magnetic fields, so north is always "true north" and it requires no adjustment.

Magnetic North

Represents the direction of the north magnetic pole from the point of observation. A compass always points to magnetic north, which moves slightly west each year due to the earth's rotation and continental drift.

Magnetic Variation

Errors in magnetic compass readings caused by variance in the earth's magnetic field at different locations on the planet. Navigational charts list the variation and a yearly level of increase. Your GPS receiver is unaffected by magnetic variation.

Map Display/Page

This is the screen you'll spend the most time consulting when navigating with a GPS receiver that has a built-in basemap or can display map data downloaded from a CD-ROM. You can watch yourself moving in real time through an electronic representation of the area around you that includes various map features.

Map Features

The physical components, such as terrain, vegetation and hydrography (water) and the cultural, or man-made features, such as buildings, roads or trails, or marine navigation aids that appear on most topographic maps and sea charts.

Map Projection

The systematic arrangement of the earth's spherical or geographic coordinate system onto a flat plane; the process of transforming a globe into a flat map with the least amount of distortion.

Mask Angle

The minimum acceptable satellite elevation above the horizon to avoid blockage of line-of-sight. Different GPS receivers have different mask angles to pick up satellite signals low on the horizon, but such signals are of lower quality because they're subject to more atmospheric disturbance.

Mean Sea Level

The average level of the ocean's surface. Used as a standard in determining land elevation or sea depths.

Meridian

A line of latitude.

Multi-Channel Receiver

A GPS receiver that can simultaneously track more than one satellite signal. Most GPS receivers now have 12 channels, but in the past single-channel receivers were the norm. These older receivers were much slower and less accurate under certain conditions, especially in tree cover where they often didn't work at all.

Multipath Error

A variance caused when a satellite signal bounces around before reaching your GPS receiver, usually off buildings.

Multiplexing Receiver

An older GPS receiver design that allowed the unit to track many satellites using fewer channels by jumping from one signal to the other and back again. Typically, multiplexing receivers require more time for satellite acquisition, work poorly under dense cover and are not as accurate as parallel-channel receivers.

N

National Marine Electronics Association (NMEA) Standard

A U.S. standards committee that defines how data is passed back and forth between pieces of electronic equipment aboard ships. Your GPS receiver is NMEA compliant.

National Oceanic and Atmospheric Administration (NOAA)

This organization is responsible for making and maintaining navigational charts in all U.S. waters, and for forecasting weather.

Nautical Mile

A unit of length used in sea and air navigation, based on the length of one minute of arc of a great circle, a little bigger than a statute mile (about 6,076 feet/1.85 km).

Navigation

The act of determining the course or heading of movement. This movement could be for a plane, ship, automobile, person on foot or any other similar means.

Navigation Message

The information transmitted by each GPS satellite containing system time, clock-correction parameters, ionospheric delay model parameters and the satellite's ephemeris data and health. The information is used to process GPS signals to give the user time, position and velocity. Also known as the data message.

NAVSTAR

The government-selected acronym for GPS satellites: NAVigation Satellite Timing And Ranging.

North-Up Orientation

Orients the GPS receiver's map display so north is always fixed at the top of the screen. You can also change your map display so that the course or track is fixed at the top.

O

Orienteering

A sport enjoyed by people who navigate with a compass around a course. Using a GPS receiver would be cheating.

Orienting Arrow

On a compass, the red- or black-outlined arrow. Used to determine bearing and the direction of magnetic north.

P

Parallel-Channel Receiver

See Multi-Channel Receiver.

Pixel

A single display element or dot on an LCD screen. The more pixels, the higher the resolution and easier to see features on an electronic map.

Plotter Page

Before electronic maps became so popular, GPS receivers had plotter pages instead of map displays. The plotter looks like a bull's-eye target, with you at the center and the rings set at regular intervals. You can see nearby waypoints in relation to your position, in addition to your recorded track log, but that's about it.

Position

An exact, unique location based on a geographic coordinate system.

Position Fix

The GPS receiver's computed position coordinates. Using a map and compass, you can get a position fix visually, by referencing the terrain and comparing it to contour lines and other map features and then triangulating.

Position Format

The way in which the GPS receiver's position is displayed on the screen. Commonly displayed as latitude/longitude in degrees and minutes, with options for degrees, minutes and seconds; degrees only; or one of several grid formats.

Position Page

One of the primary navigation pages or screens that shows the basics about your present position and, most importantly, latitude and longitude.

Precision Code (P-code)

The precise code of the GPS signal used only by the U.S. military. It is encrypted and reset every seven days.

Prime Meridian

The zero meridian, used as a reference line from which longitude to the east and west is measured. It passes through Greenwich, England.

Q

Quadrangle

A four-sided area bounded by parallels of latitude and meridians of longitude, used as a unit in mapping. A single quadrangle, or "quad" as it's popularly known, is the area shown on a standard topographic sheet published by the USGS.

R

Range

How far away something is from a fixed point, such as the distance between a starting and an ending waypoint of a route, or between a GPS satellite and receiver.

Relief

Changes in terrain; elevations or depressions in the land. See Topography.

Relief Shading

A technique for showing the relief of a landscape, its ups and downs, on a topographic map. The process makes land look three-dimensional by the use of graded shadows. Traditionally, maps are shaded as though the light source is coming from the northwest.

Ridge

A long, narrow stretch of high ground.

Route

A group of waypoints linked together to form a line between two points. The line doesn't have to be straight and the waypoints are ordered according to the direction you want to travel. Once pro-grammed into your GPS receiver, the route can be navigated forward through the waypoints or in reverse order.

RS-232

A serial input/output standard that allows data to pass back and forth between communication equipment made by various manu-facturers.

S

Saddle

A dip between hilltops or along the crest of a ridge.

Satellite Status Page

This is the page, or screen, you see after turning on your GPS and passing the legal information. It shows what satellites are in view and assigns a status bar to show signal strength and whether you have a 2D or 3D fix. The bars are always going up and down, going from clear to black, as satellites zoom over the horizon and new ones take their place. Some GPS receivers also calculate a DOP (or GDOP) and EPE value for your present position and display it on this page.

Selective Availability (SA)

This is what gave GPS receivers a bad reputation for many years. SA refers to the DoD's policy of intentionally degrading the accuracy of the satellite signals to keep them from being used with any precision by potential enemies—and subsequently, by the people who paid for the system in the first place, you and me. GPS receivers could be off the mark by as much as 300 feet (91 m) thanks to SA. SA was discontinued in May 2000 and that same receiver now might be off by a maximum of only 45 feet (14 m).

Scale

The distance between two points on a map as it relates to the distance between those same points on the earth. A map in large scale (e.g., 1:5,000) covers a smaller area in greater detail. A small-scale map (e.g., 1:1,000,000) covers a larger surface area in less detail.

Shading

An object that blocks a GPS satellite signal is said to be "shading" it. A shaded signal cannot be used to compute your location until you are past the shading object. This might be difficult if the object is overhead, like dense foliage, or exceptionally large, like a mountain.

Sighting Line

A visual line between you and some feature of the landscape that you use to take a bearing.

Slope

When land deviates from the horizontal plane it has slope. On a topographic map, the closer the contour lines are placed together, the steeper the slope. When contour lines are closer together at the top than they are at the bottom of a land feature, the slope is concave in shape. When the contour lines are farther apart on top of a land feature and closer together at the bottom, the slope is convex in shape.

Space Segment

The satellite portion of the three-segment Global Positioning System.

Speed Over Ground (SOG)

The actual speed the GPS unit is moving over the ground. This may differ from airspeed or nautical speed due to such things as headwinds or sea conditions. For example, a plane that is going 120 knots into a 10-knot headwind will have an SOG of 110 knots.

Spur

A small ridge.

Static Positioning

Position fixing when the GPS receiver's antenna—and you—are standing still, allowing for the use of position averaging techniques that improve accuracy of waypoints.

Statute Mile

A standard mile as your car's odometer measures it, 5,280 feet or 1,760 yards (1,609 meters). Slightly shorter than a nautical mile.

Straight-Line Navigation

Going from one waypoint to another in a direct line. When a waypoint is activated your GPS receiver draws a straight, dotted line to it from your present position. That line is the shortest, most direct route but often-times an impossible one. Your GPS receiver doesn't take into account any potentially dangerous obstacles that might be in your path, such as lakes, cliffs, grizzly bears, sandbars, street construction, buildings and so on.

T

Topography

Relief of the landscape; the graphic portrayal of that relief in map form by the use of contour lines.

Track (TRK)

Your current direction of travel relative to a ground position (same as Course Over Ground).

Track Log

See Breadcrumb Trail.

Track-Up Orientation

Orients your GPS receiver's map display so the current track heading is fixed at the top of the screen.

Triangulation

A method of determining the location of an unknown point, as in GPS navigation, by using the laws of plane trigonometry. Without a map and compass you can take bearings on two or more known terrain fea-tures, then plot those bearings as lines on a corresponding map. Where the lines intersect is where you are, approximately. As with satellite geometry, triangulation works best when three or more features are used to take bearings, and the features are spaced reasonably far apart.

True North

The direction of the geographic North Pole from your current position. See Magnetic North.

U

Universal Time Coordinated (UTC)

Replaced Greenwich Mean Time (GMT) as the world standard for time in 1986. UTC uses atomic clock measurements to add or omit leap seconds each year to compensate for changes in the rotation of the earth.

Universal Transverse Mercator (UTM)

Becoming more and more popular among backcountry users, UTM is easier to use than the more common Lat/Lon coordinate system, and now UTM grids can be found on most all USGS quad maps. The UTM coordinate system uses north and east distance measurements (meters), rather than time measurements as with Lat/Lon measurements, so no confusing conversions to distance are necessary. Each UTM zone is divided into a grid, and coordinates within that grid are referred to as "eastings" and "northings."

User Interface

Without a good user interface, your GPS receiver is just a fancy calculator. It only deals with numbers. Early GPS receivers were bulky bricks with a tiny screen that displayed a few lines of alphanumeric text. There were no maps, no graphic representations of compass needles or bar graphs. Next to receiver design, nothing is more important than a GPS receiver's user interface. Most of us prefer simple, clear, easy-to-read pages that tell us what we need to know and little else. Manipulating electronic maps should be intuitive and not require a lot of hunting through submenus. Naming waypoints shouldn't be an exercise in excessive button pushing. Be sure to thoroughly examine a GPS receiver's user interface before buying it.

User Segment

The portion of the three-segment Global Positioning System that includes the GPS receiver and you, the operator.

V

Velocity Made Good (VMG)

The rate of closure to a destination that compensates for variances in speed and direction. For example, you may be walking a steady 5 mph (8 kmph), but not in a straight line to your destination, in which case your VMG and speed readings will be different. VMG is a truer indication of the speed being made to the selected waypoint because it accounts for real-world conditions that put you off a straight line to your destination.

W

Waterproof

Most GPS receivers claim some degree of water resistance. The manufacturer may say its unit is weatherproof, waterproof, weather resistant, submersible and so on. But none of these terms mean anything unless the manufacturer specifies exactly what standard was used in testing the GPS receiver. For instance, if the GPS receiver has been tested according to IEC 529 IPX-7, it can withstand accidental immersion in 10 feet (3 m) of water for 30 minutes, which is pretty good. Most GPS units work fine in the rain as long as they get stowed away periodically to dry off.

Waypoint

A specific electronic address or location worth recording and storing in your GPS receiver to which you may later want to return. These may be significant ground features that rarely change from year to year (home, river crossing, marina) or temporary yet important locations (tree stand, truck, campsite).

WGS-84

World Geodetic System, 1984. The primary map datum used by GPS receivers.

Wide Area Augmentation System (WAAS)

First designed for pilots to aid in precision approaches to airports, WAAS works like DGPS does for boaters, except that it uses satellites instead of land-based beacons to transmit correction messages. A WAAS-enabled GPS receiver is accurate to within 15 feet (4.5 m) and requires no additional equipment. Because WAAS was designed for airplanes flying high over the terrain, its two satellites are in geosynchronous orbit above the equator. That means WAAS signals can be easily blocked by terrain the farther north you go. It's not uncommon for WAAS-enabled units to temporarily lose the WAAS signal, especially in wooded areas.

X

XTE/XTK

See Crosstrack Error.

Z

Zoom

Most GPS receivers have dedicated keys that let you zoom in and out of the map display, increasing or decreasing the scope and complexity of the information portrayed.

International Waterproof Ratings

The following waterproof ratings are a good way to verify exactly how good your unit is, when it comes to getting dunked!

IEC 529

The International Electrotechnical Commission's Publication 60529 (IEC 529) standard, used by the European Union, is becoming more popular. A graduated scale from 1 to 8 specifies how well an enclosure or case keeps water from getting in. That's what the "IP" ("ingress protection") part of the rating system refers to. The higher the IP number, the more "waterproof" the gadget.

IEC 529 ratings:

• IPX-1 (rain resistant): Falling water equal to ⅛- to ³⁄₁₆-inch (3- to 5-mm) rainfall per minute for 10 minutes

• IPX-2 (slanting rain): Falling water when equipment is held at a 15-degree angle

• IPX-3 (spray resistant): Spraying water, 11 gallons (38 l) per minute for 5 minutes

• IPX-4 (splash resistant): Splashing water. Same as IPX-3 but water is sprayed at all angles

• IPX-5 (jetting water): Jetting water from all angles, 3 gallons (11 l) per minute for 3 minutes from 10 feet (3 m) away

• IPX-6 (heavy seas): Water jetted from all angles, 26 gallons (98 l) per minute for 3 minutes from 10 feet (3 m) away

• IPX-7 (immersion): Dunkable for 30 minutes at a depth of 3 feet (1 m)

• IPX-8 (fish): Jacques Cousteau was personally rated at this grade

JIS2-8

The Japanese Industrial Standards (JIS) waterproof ratings are used all over the world. JIS utilizes a graduated scale similar to the IEC "IPX" scale to rate how well a piece of equipment is protected against water getting inside its case. In fact, JIS-7 and EIC IPX-7 grades for immersion are the same.

JIS ratings:

- JIS-0 (Don't even sneeze on it)

- JIS-1 (drip resistant): Withstands dripping water

- JIS-2 (light rain resistant): Dripping water when equipment is held at a 15-degree angle

- JIS-3 (spray resistant): Water sprayed at angles up to 60 degrees

- JIS-4 (splash resistant): Splashing water from any direction

- JIS-5 (hose resistant): Jetting water from any direction for 3 minutes

- JIS-6 (watertight): Powerfully jetting water from any direction for 3 minutes won't enter the case

- JIS-7 (immersion): Water won't enter the case when equipment is immersed in 3 feet (1 m) of water for 30 minutes

- JIS-8 (like a submarine!): Equipment made for continuous use underwater

USCG CFR-46

Some GPS manufacturers, especially those that sell mainly to the marine market, often advertise that their electronics hold up to "USCG CFR-46." The "USCG" part of the name stands for U.S. Coast Guard. And the "CFR-46" part refers to the Code of Federal Regulations, Title 46.

This standard isn't as precise as the graduated scales of the EIC or JIS standards, but it might fall somewhere around Grade 6 on either scale. The test calls for 65 gallons (246 l) of water per minute sprayed from any direction through a 1-inch (2.5-cm) nozzle from 10 feet (3 m) away for at least 5 minutes.

CFR-46 rating:

- CFR-46: Watertight, but cannot be immersed in water.

MIL-STD 810

Many companies that make equipment for outdoor use like to brag that their products adhere to rugged, military "MIL-STD 810" standards. Sounds impressive, right? If it's good enough for the Marines, it's good enough for me. Let's take a closer look at what this term means.

First developed for the Air Force more than forty years ago, MIL-STD 810 isn't a specific test. It's a 540-page tome that explains procedures for testing complicated military equipment. Suffice it to say, if a product is advertised as having been tested according to MIL-STD 810, it doesn't mean a thing.

MIL-STD 810 covers lots of different kinds of tests for vibration, temperature, altitude, shock resistance, dust and so on. Saying that a gadget is "waterproof" according to "MIL-STD 800 specifications" doesn't mean much either. If the manufacturer doesn't give details of how the test was performed (how deep and how long was the unit immersed?) or at least give a reference to the particular procedure used to test the equipment, then ignore any reference to MIL-STD 810.

NEMA

You won't find many GPS receivers that use the National Electronic Manufacturers Association (NEMA) rating system, but it's possible so I'll include it here. The system is suited more for rating electronics that weren't designed for extended outdoor use, such as home entertainment systems. It classifies gadgets according to indoor and outdoor use, for instance, and there's no precise definition separating what a "drip" might be, versus a "splash."

NEMA ratings:

• Type 2 (indoor): Dripping and light splashing

• Types 3, 3R, 3S: Falling rain, sleet, snow and exterior formation of ice

• Types 4, 4X: Falling rain, sleet, snow, splashing water, jetting water and exterior formation of ice

• Types 5, 12, 12X (indoor and outdoor): Dripping and light splashing

• Types 6, 6P: Jetting water, temporary and prolonged submersion at a limited depth and exterior formation of ice

• Type 13 (indoor): Spraying, splashing and water seepage, oil and non-corrosive coolants

Manufacturer
Source List

Brunton
620 E. Monroe Ave.
Riverton, WY 82501
1-800-443-4871
www.brunton.com

Cobra Electronics Corp.
6500 W. Cortland St.
Chicago, IL 60707
773-889-8870
http://www.cobra.com

DeLorme
Two DeLorme Dr.
P.O. Box 298
Yarmouth, ME 04096
800-561-5105
www.delorme.com

Fugawi
Northport Systems, Inc.
95 St. Clair Ave. W., Suite 1406
Toronto, Ontario
M4V 1N6 Canada
416-920-9300
www.fugawi.com

Garmin USA
1200 E. 151st St.
Olathe, KS 66062
913-397-8200
www.garmin.com

GPS Outfitters
P.O. Box 237
Stephens City, VA 22655
800-477-4868
www.gpsoutfitters.com

Lowrance Electronics
12000 E. Skelly Dr.
Tulsa, Oklahoma 74128
800-324-1356
www.lowrance.com

Magellan Systems Corporation
960 Overland Ct.
San Dimas, CA 91773
909-394-5000
www.thalesnavigation.com

Maptech
10 Industrial Way
Amesbury, MA 01913
978-792-1000
www.maptech.com

National Geographic Maps
P.O. Box 4537
Evergreen, CO 80437-4357
1-800-962-1643
www.nationalgeographic.com

National Oceanic and Atmospheric Administration (NOAA)
14th St. & Constitution Ave. NW
  Room 6217
Washington, D.C. 20230
202-482-6090
www.noaa.gov

Pharos Science and Applications
411 Amapola Dr.
Torrance, CA 90501
310-212-7088
www.pharosgps.com

U.S. Geological Survey
Headquarters, John W. Powell
  Federal Building
12201 Sunrise Valley Dr.
Reston, Virginia 20192
703-648-4054
www.usgs.gov

Index

U

Universal Transverse Mercator (UTM), 69, 76–79, 82, 84, 90–93, 130

United States Coast Guard, 35, 36, 123

United States Geographic Survey (USGS) Map, 25, 48, 54, 55, 58, 59, 63–69, 71, 76, 81–84, 90, 94, 98, 129, 132–133, 138, 139

V

Vector Map, 131–133, 138

Velocity Made Good (VMG), 57

W

Waterproof, 126–127

Waypoint, 19, 23, 40, 46, 49, 50, 52, 53, 54, 55, 56, 57, 59, 79, 87, 90, 92, 93, 96, 97, 99, 100, 102, 103, 105, 108, 109, 112–119, 123, 124–126, 139, 140, 147–148

Weather, 96–97, 119–121

Wide Area Augmentation System (WAAS), 30–33, 40, 43, 45, 146–147

World Geodetic Survey 1984 (WGS-84), 70–72, 124

Z

Zoom Level, 52, 96, 119

Creative Publishing international
is your complete source of how-to information for the outdoors

HUNTING BOOKS
- Advanced Turkey Hunting
- Advanced Whitetail Hunting
- Bowhunting Equipment & Skills
- The Complete Guide to Hunting
- Dog Training
- Duck Hunting
- Elk Hunting
- Hunting Record-Book Bucks
- Mule Deer Hunting
- Muzzleloading
- Pronghorn Hunting
- Whitetail Hunting
- Whitetail Techniques & Tactics
- Wild Turkey

FISHING BOOKS
- Advanced Bass Fishing
- The Art of Freshwater Fishing
- The Complete Guide to Freshwater Fishing
- Fishing for Catfish
- Fishing Rivers & Streams
- Fishing Tips & Tricks
- Fishing with Artificial Lures
- Inshore Salt Water Fishing
- Kids Gone Fishin'
- Largemouth Bass
- Modern Methods of Ice Fishing
- Northern Pike & Muskie
- Offshore Salt Water Fishing
- Panfish
- Salt Water Fishing Tactics
- Smallmouth Bass
- Striped Bass Fishing: Salt Water Strategies
- Successful Walleye Fishing
- Trout

FLY FISHING BOOKS
- The Art of Fly Tying
- The Art of Fly Tying – CD ROM
- Fishing Dry Flies – Surface Presentations for Trout in Streams
- Fishing Nymphs, Wet Flies & Streamers – Subsurface Techniques for Trout in Streams
- Fly-Fishing Equipment & Skills
- Fly Fishing for Trout in Streams
- Fly Fishing for Beginners
- Fly-Tying Techniques & Patterns

COOKBOOKS
- America's Favorite Fish Recipes
- America's Favorite Wild Game Recipes
- Babe & Kris Winkleman's Great Fish & Game Recipes
- Cooking Wild in Kate's Camp
- Cooking Wild in Kate's Kitchen
- Dressing & Cooking Wild Game
- Game Bird Cookery
- The New Cleaning & Cooking Fish
- Preparing Fish & Wild Game
- The Saltwater Cookbook
- Venison Cookery

To purchase these or other Creative Publishing international titles, contact your local bookseller, or visit our website at
www.creativepub.com